BUILDING A BUSINESS ABROAD

HOW TO ENJOY A LIFE OF PROFIT AND PURPOSE ANYWHERE IN THE WORLD

JAMILIA GRIER

ISBN (Paperback): ISBN: 979-8-9921143-5-5
ISBN (Ebook): 979-8-9921143-0-0

Published by The Real Expat
A division of ByteBao L.L.C—F.Z.
Meydan Freezone, Dubai, United Arab Emirates
www.therealexpat.com

Printed in the United States of America (for paperback edition)

Disclaimer:
Unless otherwise indicated, all names, characters, businesses, places, events, and incidents in this book are either the product of the author's imagination or used in a fictitious manner. Any resemblance to actual persons, living or dead, or actual events is purely coincidental.

This book is intended for informational purposes only and does not constitute professional advice. The author and publisher disclaim any liability arising directly or indirectly from the use of this material.

The author asserts their moral right to be identified as the creator of this work.

For permissions requests, contact hello@jamiliagrier.com

Digital Rights Management (DRM):
This ebook is protected by Amazon's Kindle DRM to prevent unauthorized sharing and copying. It can only be accessed through authorized Amazon devices or applications.

Table of Contents

Introduction

Imagine waking up each day to a thriving business that seamlessly integrates with your lifestyle, where every task feels purposeful and enjoyable. But it gets better. Imagine this life taking place in a country where you've always dreamed of living, free from the constraints of a traditional 9-to-5 job. This isn't just a fantasy—it's a reality that's more achievable than ever before.

Years after the global pandemic, we all know that tomorrow is not promised to us. If your life was not affected, you probably saw friends or family experiencing situations they never could have expected. The security of cushy jobs and fat paychecks vanished overnight, leaving countless individuals searching for meaning and stability. I understand this firsthand. Even with the highest-paying job of my life post-COVID, I felt an emptiness that I could no longer ignore. That inner voice urging me towards something more became impossible to silence.

Are you tired of watching others live exciting, unbounded lives abroad while you're tethered to a desk? Perhaps you're an expat grappling with a new culture, but yearning to turn your entrepreneurial dreams into reality. Perhaps you're just about to take a life-changing leap, but the fear of financial uncertainty is holding you back. Wherever you are on this journey, this book is for you.

This guide is for dreamers and doers—those who aspire to craft an international life and build something meaningful. Whether you're already overseas or still planning your exodus, you don't need to have all the answers right now. What you need is a roadmap from someone who has navigated this path before, armed with tools to help you create a life of freedom and fulfillment.

In these pages, you'll discover how to build a business that operates around your ideal lifestyle, not the other way around. You'll learn to balance ambition with well-being, turning profit into purpose. This isn't just about starting a business; it's about crafting a life where work feels like play, where your passion fuels your success, and where you can thrive in any corner of the globe.

Three years ago, I was living in one of Singapore's most coveted neighborhoods, gazing out at the stunning waters of Sentosa. My life appeared perfect. But I felt a profound emptiness. This was my reality—a mother of four, living what many would consider a dream expat life, yet grappling with a persistent sense that I was missing my true calling.

As someone who has called four different countries home, I've experienced firsthand the unique challenges and opportunities that come with building a life and business abroad. Every morning over a decade of living abroad, as I looked out over various skylines, a small voice inside me grew louder. It whispered of untapped potential, of a desire to help others, of a life purpose not yet fulfilled.

It was in one of these moments of reflection that I made a decision that would alter the course of my life and career. I chose to no longer suppress the urge to start my own business. I decided to be confident in my abilities and to see my status as an expat not just as a chance to work for a company abroad, but as an opportunity to have a real impact on the world.

This book is born from that moment of clarity and the journey that followed. It's not the work of an armchair expert or a theorist. Every page is filled with hard-won wisdom gained through doing—through the sacrifices I've made, the challenges I've overcome, and the successes I've achieved as a mother of four building businesses across multiple countries.

I wrote this book because it's the guide I desperately wished for during my journey. When I was navigating the complexities of entrepreneurship in foreign lands while balancing family life, I longed for a resource that offered real, practical advice from someone who had walked this path before.

Within these pages, you'll find the strategies, insights, and encouragement that I've gathered through years of hands-on experience. My hope—my prayer—is that by sharing my experiences, I can help you avoid many of the pitfalls I came across and accelerate your path to success.

This book is more than just a guide, it's a testament to what's possible when you dare to pursue your dreams across borders. It's the culmination of years of trial and error, of balancing business ambitions with the needs of a growing family, of learning to thrive in new cultures while staying true to my purpose.

Whether you're standing on your own metaphorical balcony, pondering your next move, or you're already in the thick of expat entrepreneurship, consider this book your companion on the journey to creating a business and life abroad that truly fulfills you.

Let's turn that feeling of "something's missing" into the catalyst for your most exciting chapter yet. Your expat entrepreneurial adventure starts now, and I'm here to guide you every step of the way.

This is not a book about business theory

If you're looking for generic business theories, you can find those anywhere. But for actually building a business abroad, those theories often fall flat. This book is different.

This is a book about doing. Within these pages, you won't find abstract concepts or academic jargon. Instead, you'll dive into:

- **My personal stories**: Raw, honest accounts of the challenges I've faced and overcome while living and building businesses across four different countries.

- **Understandable case studies**: Practical examples of expat entrepreneurs who've navigated the complexities of international business and come out on top.

- **Problem-solving tools**: Frameworks and approaches I've developed to overcome obstacles specific to expat entrepreneurship.

- **Actionable strategies**: Concrete tips and techniques you can implement immediately to tackle the unique challenges of running a business abroad.

This book bridges the gap between theory and practice. It's the resource I wish I had when I was starting out—a guide that doesn't just tell you what to do, but shows you how to do it, based on authentic experiences and actual results.

This is not a book about get-rich-quick schemes in exotic locations

Let's be clear: this book is absolutely about making money and building wealth. But it's not about chasing fleeting opportunities or falling for the myth of easy riches in far-flung places.

Instead, this is a guide to creating lasting, sustainable wealth—the kind that supports the lifestyle you dream of, wherever in the world you choose to live.

Here's what you'll find:

- Strategies for building businesses that generate consistent, growing profits over time

- Insights on how to create multiple streams of income that can weather economic shifts and global changes

- Approaches to wealth building that align with your values and life goals as an expat

- Real-world examples of successful expat entrepreneurs who've built enduring, profitable businesses

This book is for those who understand that true wealth usually isn't about a quick windfall, but about building something meaningful that grows over time. It's about creating a business that not only funds your expat lifestyle today, but sets you up for a prosperous future.

So if you're looking for get-rich-quick schemes, this isn't the book for you. But if you're ready to roll up your sleeves and build real, lasting wealth as an expat entrepreneur, you're in exactly the right place.

This is not a book about one-size-fits-all entrepreneurship

This book recognizes a fundamental truth that many business guides overlook: successful entrepreneurship begins with understanding yourself. It's a journey in self-discovery—and it ain't easy.

Here's what makes this book different:

- It's grounded in the reality that your business should be an extension of who you are, not a mold you force yourself into.
- We'll dive deep into the journey of self-discovery that's crucial for any aspiring expat entrepreneur.
- You'll learn how to align your business with your passions, values, and personal definition of success.

Remember, all successful entrepreneurs know who they are. You can't build the life of your dreams without first understanding what that dream looks like for you specifically.

This book is about the real work—the inner work—that leads to lasting success. It's about exploring who you are, what you love, what your passions are, and what you need as an individual.

So, if you're ready to do the deep, rewarding work of self-discovery alongside building your business, this book is for you.

This is not a book about grinding yourself to dust for success

If you're looking for another guide that glorifies the "hustle culture" or promotes working yourself to exhaustion, this isn't it. This book recognizes a fundamental truth: sustainable business success requires sustainable health.

Here's what we'll explore instead:

- Why prioritizing your health is crucial for long-term entrepreneurial success

- How to build a business that supports your well-being, not sacrifices it

- Strategies for maintaining work-life balance in the unique context of expat entrepreneurship

In these pages, you'll discover:

- Practical tips for integrating healthy habits into your entrepreneurial journey

- Ways to design your business around your ideal lifestyle, not the other way around

- Techniques for managing stress and avoiding burnout while building your venture

Remember, many people leave the corporate world precisely because they're tired of neglecting their health—the grueling travel schedules, sedentary lifestyles, and poor eating habits that come with it. This book is about breaking that cycle, not perpetuating it in a new setting.

Because here's the truth: a business that requires you to sacrifice your health isn't truly successful. This book is about building a venture that enhances your life, not depletes it.

Are you ready to go global?

In short, I want you to know one thing: if I can do this, you can too. I've been where you are now—filled with dreams, perhaps some doubts, but an undeniable drive to create something meaningful in a new land. I've navigated the complexities of living in four different countries while raising a family and building a business. I've faced the challenges, made the mistakes, and found the strategies that work.

And now, I'm here to be your guide.

This book isn't just a collection of theories or abstract concepts. It's a roadmap drawn from actual experiences, hard-won lessons, and proven successes. Together, we'll tackle the nuanced challenges of entrepreneurship abroad—from mindset shifts to social networks, from maintaining work-life balance to building sustainable profits.

Remember, your journey is unique, and that's your strength. Your experiences, your passions, your vision—these are the foundation of your success. This book will help you harness these assets and turn them into a thriving business and a fulfilling life abroad.

So, whether you're on the brink of taking the leap or already in the midst of your expat entrepreneurial adventure, know this: you have what it takes. The path ahead may not always be easy, but with the right guidance and mindset, it can be incredibly rewarding.

Are you ready to transform your expat experience into entrepreneurial success? Are you prepared to build a business that not only profits but also aligns with your values and supports your ideal lifestyle?

Let's embark on this exciting journey together. Turn the page, and let's craft your global success story.

PART I

Foundations of Freedom

CHAPTER 1:

The Expat Advantage

"Life is either a daring adventure or nothing at all."
–Helen Keller

There's a moment in every entrepreneur's life when you realize that the path you've been on no longer serves you. For some, it's a quiet knowing that seeps in over time, a whisper urging you toward something different. For others, it comes like a wave, a sudden realization that you've outgrown your current life and need something more—more freedom, more challenge, more growth.

For me, it was a bit of both. It started out very softly, almost like a gut instinct, until it grew to a booming voice I could no longer ignore. The first whisper was back in 2008 when I was a first-year associate at a law firm in Connecticut. The whisper nudged me to pitch a business development idea to the partners at my firm. *Me? A first-year associate?* The idea went against all conventional rules of hierarchy in law firms. The persistent whisper encouraged me to explore business opportunities in China, particularly for our bankruptcy and technology practice groups. In 2008, during the height of the financial crisis, our bankruptcy practice group thrived. And that small voice was pressuring me to strike while the iron was hot. So I did.

I took one of the most highly respected partners of the law firm, where I was a first-year associate on a business development trip to China. I recall standing in the gleaming lobby of a high-rise hotel in Jinan, the capital of Shandong province, my heart pounding with a mix of excitement and trepidation. It was 2009, and at 28 years old, I was about to embark on the most challenging—and potentially rewarding—week of my young legal career.

As a fresh-faced associate at one of Connecticut's prestigious law firms, I had been there barely a year when an unexpected opportunity arose. The firm's renowned bankruptcy practice was looking to expand its reach into China, tapping into the growing market of Chinese creditors seeking relief in U.S. bankruptcy courts. And somehow, I—the rookie with a background in Mandarin and a passion for Chinese culture—had been chosen to spearhead this business development trip.

My mission? To guide James Tancredi, one of our most respected partners, through a whirlwind tour of Shandong province, introducing him to key Chinese government officials and potential clients. The weight of this responsibility settled on my shoulders like a heavy cloak as I rehearsed my opening lines in Mandarin one last time.

"You've got this," I whispered to my reflection in the polished marble pillar. But did I? Doubt crept in as I recalled the meticulous planning of the past few weeks. I had crafted an ambitious itinerary filled with back-to-back meetings, conferences, formal dinners, and casual networking events. It was a delicate balance of showcasing our firm's expertise while navigating the nuances of Chinese business etiquette.

As I saw James's imposing figure emerge from the elevator, I took a deep breath. This was it. No turning back now.

The next seven days were a blur of activity. We crisscrossed Shandong, from the bustling streets of Jinan to the coastal city of Qingdao, and onto Shanghai, and continued far out west to Chengdu. In boardrooms and banquet halls, I found myself not just translating words, but bridging cultures. I moderated discussions between James and local officials, explaining the intricacies of U.S. bankruptcy law in Mandarin while simultaneously interpreting the subtle cultural cues that could make or break a potential partnership. I had never worked in that capacity before; it was frightening and thrilling at the same time.

There were moments of triumph, like when I successfully negotiated a last-minute meeting with a key official in Jinan, opening doors we thought were firmly shut. And there were near-disasters, like the time I almost used the wrong honorific for a high-ranking party member, catching myself just in time.

Through it all, I surprised myself. The nervous energy that had threatened to overwhelm me in that hotel lobby transformed into a driving force. I was in my element, switching effortlessly between languages, cultures, and contexts. I watched as Robert, initially skeptical of this young associate's abilities, began to rely on my insights and judgment.

As our trip drew to a close, sitting in a late-night strategy session with James in our hotel in Shanghai, a realization hit me with the force of a tidal wave. I had just spent a week operating far beyond the confines of my job description as a junior associate. I had been a cultural ambassador, a business developer, a strategist, and a leader.

"You know," James said, breaking the comfortable silence that had fallen between us, "I didn't know what to expect when the firm suggested sending you on this trip. But I have to say, you've opened doors here that I never thought possible. I think, one day, you will have your own office right in this city."

His words should have filled me with pride, and they did. But they also stirred something else—a restlessness, a hunger for more. I realized that while I had excelled in my role as a lawyer on this trip, what truly energized me was the challenges that fell outside the traditional bounds of legal practice.

As our plane took off from Shanghai International Airport, carrying us back to the familiar skyscrapers of New York, I gazed out at the receding coastline of China. I had come here to help expand our firm's practice, but I was leaving with an expanded vision of my own potential.

The young associate who had nervously practiced Mandarin in a hotel lobby a week ago was gone. In her place was someone who had glimpsed a future full of possibilities—possibilities that extended far beyond the walls of any law firm, no matter how prestigious.

I didn't know it then, but this trip was the first step on a path that would eventually lead me away from the safety of corporate law and toward the uncertain but thrilling world of entrepreneurship. It was in the bustling cities of Shandong that I first tasted the exhilaration of creating value beyond billable hours, of building bridges across cultures, of taking risks and seeing them pay off.

As the coast of China disappeared beneath the clouds, I made a silent promise to myself. This trip wouldn't be a one-off adventure, but the beginning of a journey. A journey to explore the full extent of my capabilities, to seek out challenges that would push me beyond my comfort zone, and to never again underestimate the power of taking a leap into the unknown.

Little did I know, this mindset—cultivated during that transformative week in China—would be the very foundation upon which I would later build my own business, fusing my legal expertise with my passion for cross-cultural communication and problem-solving.

The path ahead was far from clear, but one thing was certain: I was no longer content only practicing law. I was ready to create, to innovate, to lead. The seeds of entrepreneurship had been planted, nurtured by the rich soil of a country that had always fascinated me, and watered by the realization of my own untapped potential.

My journey as an entrepreneur had begun, not in a garage or a business school classroom, but in the unexpected crucible of a business trip to China.

The Entrepreneurial Expat: A Risk-Taker by Definition

Entrepreneurship and expat life are intertwined in ways that go far beyond surface-level similarities. Both paths demand a willingness to embrace risk, an ability to adapt quickly, and the courage to confront your deepest fears about failure, uncertainty, and success. If you've chosen to live abroad or start a business, you've already proven yourself a risk-taker, whether you recognize it is another matter. It takes a special kind of person to leave behind the comfort of the familiar, whether that's as a steady paycheck or the security of your home country.

For people like us, staying in one place—both physically and mentally—feels more like a trap than a blessing. We thrive on the challenge of the unknown, the thrill of creating something new. This mindset drives us to choose unconventional paths, turning risk-taking from a mere trait into a necessity.

My move to China was a prime example of this entrepreneurial spirit in action. One of the biggest unexpected challenges I faced was the sheer amount of language I needed to learn just to function in daily life. In my previous surroundings, I had the luxury of understanding the nuances of language and culture. But in China, even simple tasks like grocery shopping or ordering food required a level of language proficiency I hadn't anticipated. It was a humbling experience, one that taught me that to thrive, I would have to put in the work to adapt.

There was a moment when I questioned my decision to move. It wasn't any one event, but the sheer magnitude of the change—the realization that I had truly left behind everything familiar. The impact hit me harder than I expected. I ignored those doubts, focusing on the fact that this was a new beginning, not a repeat of the past. Building something new meant embracing the awkwardness of change; that's why I was there. I accepted that things wouldn't feel comfortable for a while, but that was okay. I was doing something different, and it was bound to feel different.

Living in China ultimately taught me I am far more resilient than I ever gave myself credit for. I learned I could adapt to challenges that initially felt insurmountable. Whether it was navigating the language barrier or adjusting to a new business culture, every hurdle was a reminder that I could do much more than I had ever thought possible.

These lessons would later shape how I approached business, particularly during negotiations with buyers from Angang Steel over a large iron ore purchase. Understanding the cultural differences in how business is conducted gave me an edge, and that experience reinforced the value of adaptability in both life and work.

In this chapter, we'll explore the mindset that drives people like us to choose these unconventional paths. We'll delve into how risk-taking becomes not just a trait but a necessity, and how the challenges we face as expats and entrepreneurs shape us into more resilient, adaptable, and ultimately successful individuals.

Risk-Taking as a Skill

When people think of risk, they often picture recklessness—leaping into the unknown without a plan. But real risk-taking is much more intentional. It's about understanding the stakes, weighing your options, and still choosing to move forward because the potential for growth far outweighs the fear of failure.

One of the biggest risks I took was when I transitioned from corporate life to entrepreneurship. I had a hefty salary, and as a mother of four, that financial stability was important to me. Walking away from that security wasn't an easy decision. The weight of it sat heavily on my shoulders—not just as a professional, but as a mother. I had always been used to a steady income, and suddenly I was entering a world where nothing was guaranteed.

When I first started my business in Singapore, I thought clients would come flooding in. I believed that once I launched, people would immediately recognize the value I brought to the table. But I was wrong. There was no line of clients waiting for me. I had to build my brand, establish my reputation, and go out there to speak to people—a skill I had barely exercised in my previous corporate life. It was uncomfortable, and it took a lot more time and effort than I had anticipated. But it was also one of the most valuable lessons I've ever learned: business, much like life abroad, is about building relationships and showing up, even when things don't go according to plan.

There were people in my life who questioned my decision to leave the corporate world. After all, it wasn't just me taking this risk—it was my family, too. I had to get alignment with my husband, and I'm lucky that he understood my need to start my own business. It was a financial risk, and I knew it wouldn't pay off immediately. But it was something I had to do, and in the long run, it has been worth it. My lifestyle has improved in ways I never thought possible. I go to the gym a few times a week. I have more time with my children. And I'm able to structure my life in a way that suits me—things that, for me, are incredibly valuable.

Rule: Maintain a Growth Mindset

Living abroad or starting a business forces you to cultivate a growth mindset—a belief that every challenge, every obstacle, is an opportunity to learn and grow. It's not about having all the answers upfront; it's about trusting that you can figure things out along the way.

When I moved to China, I experienced culture shock in ways I hadn't expected. Simple tasks, like grocery shopping or navigating the city, became complex endeavors due to language barriers and unfamiliar customs. In business, I faced similar moments of uncertainty when launching new initiatives or managing unexpected setbacks. But in both situations, I learned that adaptability and resilience are the keys to survival.

Having a growth mindset means embracing the fact that you will fail at times, that you will face moments where you don't know the next step. But it also means recognizing that those moments of failure are not the end—they're stepping stones on the path to success. I've learned more from my mistakes, both in life and in business, than from my successes. Each misstep has taught me something new about myself and about what it takes to thrive in uncertain environments.

As an expat and an entrepreneur, you'll face countless situations that require you to pivot, to think on your feet, and to adjust your expectations. But with a growth mindset, you can turn every challenge into an opportunity for growth. It's not about avoiding failure—it's about embracing it as part of the process.

CASE STUDY: FROM SILICON VALLEY TO SÃO PAULO STARTUP SUCCESS

Maya Patel, a 28-year-old software developer from San Francisco, had always dreamed of combining her love for tech with her passion for travel. While she enjoyed her job at a mid-sized tech company in Silicon Valley, she couldn't shake the feeling that she was missing out on bigger opportunities for growth and adventure.

When her company announced they were looking for volunteers to help set up a new office in São Paulo, Brazil, Maya saw her chance. Despite concerns from family and friends about leaving a stable job in the tech mecca of the world, Maya took the leap. She saw it not just as a career move, but as an opportunity to challenge herself in a completely new environment.

The first few months in São Paulo were a whirlwind of excitement and challenges. While Maya had studied Spanish in college, Portuguese was a new beast entirely. Simple tasks like ordering coffee or explaining her dietary restrictions became daily adventures in miscommunication. At work, she struggled to convey complex technical concepts to her new Brazilian team members, often resorting to a mix of English, rudimentary Portuguese, and elaborate hand gestures.

The work culture in Brazil also threw Maya for a loop. Used to the fast-paced, often impersonal nature of Silicon Valley, she found the relationship-focused Brazilian work style both refreshing and frustrating. Meetings that she expected to last 30 minutes often stretched to two hours as colleagues discussed weekend plans and family updates before getting down to business. Her initial attempts to stick to rigid agendas and timelines were met with gentle resistance and good-natured teasing about the "American obsession with efficiency."

Despite these challenges, Maya was determined to make the most of her expat experience. She threw herself into Portuguese lessons, practiced with patient Uber drivers, and even started a language exchange meetup group for tech professionals. She began keeping a journal, not just of her language progress, but of her cultural observations and the many times she had to laugh at herself for a social faux pas.

As Maya became more comfortable with the language and culture, she noticed gaps in the local tech scene. While São Paulo had a growing startup ecosystem, many promising ideas struggled to get off the ground due to a lack of technical expertise or difficulty in adapting Silicon Valley models to the Brazilian market.

The idea of starting her own tech consultancy took root in Maya's mind. She envisioned a company that could bridge the gap between Silicon Valley know-how and Brazilian business realities. However, the thought of leaving her stable job to start a business in a foreign country was daunting. She spent weeks researching the market, networking with local entrepreneurs, and seeking advice from mentors back home.

After six months of deliberation, Maya made the bold decision to resign from her job and start her own company. She had saved enough to sustain herself for a year and had built a solid network in São Paulo's tech community. Still, as she submitted her resignation letter, she felt a mix of excitement and sheer terror.

The early days of Maya's startup, which she named "TechPonte" (Tech Bridge in Portuguese), were challenging. She struggled with Brazil's notorious bureaucracy, spending countless hours navigating unfamiliar legal and tax systems. There were days when she questioned her decision, especially when potential clients ghosted her or when she encountered unexpected regulatory hurdles.

But Maya's experiences as an expat had taught her resilience and adaptability. She approached each setback as a problem to be solved, rather than a reason to give up. When she struggled to explain her business model in Portuguese, she hired a business language coach. When she realized she lacked knowledge about local business customs, she joined a mentorship program for foreign entrepreneurs in Brazil.

Maya's breakthrough came three months into her venture when she landed a contract with a promising FinTech startup to develop a mobile payment system tailored for Brazil's unbanked population. The project was challenging, requiring Maya to work long hours and constantly communicate with the client to understand the unique needs of Brazilian consumers. But it was also exhilarating. For the first time, Maya felt she was creating something truly impactful, not just adding features to existing products.

The success of this project led to referrals, and slowly, TechPonte grew. Maya hired her first employees, a diverse team of Brazilian and international talent. She fostered a culture that blended the best aspects of Silicon Valley innovation with the warmth and creativity she appreciated in Brazilian culture.

One year into her entrepreneurial journey, Maya faced her biggest challenge yet. A well-funded competitor from the U.S. announced they were entering the Brazilian market with a similar service. For a moment, Maya felt overwhelmed, fearing that everything she had built would be swept away.

But then she remembered how far she had come, how much she had already overcome. Instead of giving up, Maya saw this as an opportunity to innovate. She gathered her team for a marathon brainstorming session, fueled by plenty of pão de queijo and cafezinho. They emerged with a plan to pivot their services, focusing on helping traditional Brazilian businesses digitize their operations, a niche the U.S. competitor had overlooked.

This unique approach resonated with their target market. Even as the competitor entered the market, TechPonte continued to grow. Two years after starting her company, Maya's business was thriving. She had a team of fifteen employees, a stable client base, and was even beginning to explore opportunities in other Latin American countries.

Reflecting on her journey, Maya realized how much she had changed. The once-cautious software developer from San Francisco had transformed into a confident, adaptable entrepreneur. She had learned to embrace uncertainty, to see challenges as opportunities, and to trust in her ability to navigate unfamiliar territories.

Maya's expat experience had been the catalyst for her entrepreneurial journey, pushing her out of her comfort zone and forcing her to develop a growth mindset. The skills she had gained–adaptability, resilience, cross-cultural communication—had been invaluable in her entrepreneurial venture.

As Maya looked to the future, she felt a sense of excitement rather than fear. She knew there would be more challenges ahead, but she also knew that she had developed the mindset and skills to face them. Her journey as an entrepreneurial expat had only just begun, and she couldn't wait to see where it would take her next.

Four Key Mindset Lessons from Maya's Journey

- **Embrace Uncertainty**: Maya's decision to leave her comfortable job in Silicon Valley for an unknown future in São Paulo demonstrates the power of viewing uncertainty as an opportunity rather than a threat. This open mindset allowed her to discover new possibilities she might have otherwise missed.

- **Cultivate Adaptability**: Throughout her journey, Maya faced numerous challenges, from language barriers to unfamiliar business practices. Her ability to adapt, rather than resist these differences, was crucial to her success. This flexible mindset turned potential obstacles into stepping stones for growth.

- **Maintain a Growth Perspective**: Maya consistently approached new situations as opportunities to learn and improve. Whether it was mastering Portuguese or understanding local market needs, she saw every experience as a chance to expand her skills and knowledge. This growth mindset was key to her personal and professional development.

- **Foster Innovative Thinking**: When faced with strong competition, Maya innovated rather than retreat. By pivoting her business model to address a niche market, she demonstrated the power of creative problem-solving. This innovation-focused mindset enabled her to turn challenges into unique business opportunities.

Take a Moment to Reflect

Now that we've explored the entrepreneurial expat mindset, let's dive deeper into how you can cultivate and strengthen these attributes in your own life. The following reflection questions and action steps are designed to help you embrace uncertainty, cultivate adaptability, maintain a growth perspective, and foster innovative thinking.

Reflection Questions:

1. Think about a time when you faced significant uncertainty in your life or career. How did you react? What thoughts and emotions did you experience?

2. Recall a situation where you had to adapt to a new environment or circumstance. What strategies did you use? What challenges did you face, and what did you learn about yourself in the process?

3. Consider your personal growth over the past year. What new skills or knowledge have you acquired? How did you approach learning in these areas?

4. Reflect on a current problem in your personal or professional life. How have you been approaching it so far? Have you considered any unconventional solutions?

5. Which of the four mindset attributes (embracing uncertainty, cultivating adaptability, maintaining a growth perspective, fostering innovative thinking) come most naturally to you? Which is the most challenging?

Take Action:

- **Uncertainty Embrace Challenge**: This week, intentionally put yourself in a small, uncertain situation. This could be trying a new food, taking a different route to work, or starting a conversation with a stranger. After the experience, journal about how it felt and what you learned.

- **Adaptability Experiment**: Choose one aspect of your daily routine and change it for a week. This could be waking up an hour earlier, adopting a new exercise routine, or changing your work environment. At the end of the week, reflect on how you adapted to this change.

- **Growth Mindset Project**: Identify a skill you've always wanted to learn but have been putting off. Commit to spending fifteen minutes a day for the next week learning about or practicing this skill. At the end of the week, reflect on your progress and learning.

- **Innovation Brainstorm:** Choose one everyday object in your home or office. For 5 minutes, list as many alternative uses for this object as you can think of. Don't censor yourself–the goal is quantity, not quality. Afterwards, reflect on how it felt to think creatively.

By engaging with these reflections and actions, you'll strengthen your entrepreneurial expat mindset. Remember, developing these attributes is an ongoing process. The goal is not perfection, but progress. Each small step you take is moving you closer to embodying the mindset of a successful entrepreneurial expat.

As you work through these exercises, pay attention to how your perspective shifts. Notice the opportunities that appear as you embrace uncertainty, cultivate adaptability, maintain a growth perspective, and foster innovative thinking. These are the foundations upon which you'll build your unique journey as an entrepreneurial expat.

In the next chapter, we'll explore how to break free from conventional wisdom and chart your own course—one that's as unique as you are. The mindset you're developing now will be crucial as you navigate that process.

CHAPTER 2

Breaking Free for Bigger Dreams

"You never change your life until you step out of your comfort zone; change begins at the end of your comfort zone."

–Roy T. Bennett

The view from my balcony in Sentosa was nothing short of spectacular. Lush palm trees swayed gently in the breeze, framing a picturesque marina filled with sleek private yachts. The azure waters of the Singapore Strait stretched to the horizon, meeting a cloudless sky in a seamless blend of blue. This was Sentosa, one of Singapore's most affluent neighborhoods, and I called it home.

As I stood there, taking in the immaculate landscaping, the pristine beaches, and the air of exclusivity that permeated every corner of this island paradise, I couldn't help but feel a sense of irony. Here I was, living in what many would consider a slice of heaven, and yet I felt more confined than ever.

It was 2019, and I had recently been appointed as the Global Head of Data Privacy and Operations at Standard Chartered Bank. The title itself was a mouthful, matched only by the scope of my responsibilities. I had just finished assembling a team of over 50 data privacy professionals, spread across continents, all looking to me for leadership and direction.

On paper, I had it all. A prestigious global role at a major international bank. A salary that allowed me to live in one of Singapore's most coveted addresses. The flexibility to work from home, balancing my professional life with personal time in this oasis of luxury. I could afford almost anything I wanted–fancy dinners at waterfront restaurants, weekends at exclusive beach clubs, the latest gadgets. By all conventional measures, I had "made it."

And yet, as I turned away from the postcard-perfect view and sat down at my desk, staring at a screen filled with endless emails and meeting invites, I felt an inexplicable emptiness gnawing at me.

My phone buzzed–a message from my mother back in the States. "So proud of you, honey! You've come so far." I smiled, but it felt forced. Yes, I had come far, geographically and professionally, but was it in the right direction?

Later that evening, as I took a leisurely stroll along the private beach near my home, the juxtaposition of my external success and internal turmoil became even more stark. The soft sand under my feet, the gentle lapping of waves, the distant laughter from a nearby resort–it was all so perfect. Too perfect. Each step on this idyllic beach felt like a step further away from my true self, my real aspirations.

As I watched the sun dip below the horizon, painting the sky in brilliant hues of orange and pink, I couldn't shake the feeling that while I had achieved the lifestyle many people dream of, I was somehow missing out on living. The golden cage I had built for myself was undeniably beautiful, but it was still a cage.

Later that evening, at a dinner party with fellow expats and banking executives, the conversation flowed as smoothly as the expensive wine. Talk of market trends, corporate strategies, and the next big career moves filled the air. I nodded along, playing the part of the successful executive, all the while an inner voice screamed for something more.

As I drove home that night, the glittering lights of Singapore's financial district seemed to mock me. Each towering skyscraper, each neon sign, felt like a reminder of the golden cage I had built for myself.

Back in my apartment, I stood on the balcony, letting the warm tropical air wash over me. I thought about the journey that had brought me here–the long hours, the sacrifices, the relentless climb up the corporate ladder. I had achieved everything I thought I wanted, everything society had told me to strive for. So why did it feel so... empty?

The next day, in the middle of a global conference call, it hit me. As I listened to discussions about compliance regulations and operational efficiencies, I realized I wasn't just bored. I was in the wrong place entirely. My mind wandered to the side-projects I'd been tinkering with, ideas for a blockchain startup that I gave up on due to my day job. For the first time, I allowed myself to really envision a different path.

Over the next few weeks, that vision became clearer. I found myself staying up late, not to answer work emails, but to research entrepreneurship, to sketch out business plans, to connect with startup founders. The more I explored, the more alive I felt. It was as if a part of me that had been dormant for years was finally awakening.

But with this awakening came the weight of expectation. How could I walk away from this prestigious role? What would my team think? My family? The colleagues who had supported my rise through the ranks? The thought of disappointing them was almost unbearable.

I remember the day I finally decided. I was at lunch with my boss and another executive at the bank. We were going around the table talking about our previous careers. When the conversation reached me and it was time for me to talk about my past professional life, it sounded like something from out of a movie. Brokering trade deals with Chinese manufacturers, speaking Chinese and having an insight into both business and culture. Suddenly, I felt like an imposter. Everyone's face was shocked, until finally one of the men asked me bluntly, "So why are you here?"

I smiled sheepishly. "I don't know," I replied. I shrugged and continued my meal like the question didn't bother me. But it did.

That evening, I shared the story with my husband and floated my decision to leave the bank and pursue entrepreneurship. The silence that followed felt eternal. Then, my husband said: "Are you sure about this? You've worked so hard to get where you are."

I took a deep breath. "I am sure," I said, surprising myself with the conviction in my voice. "I've worked hard to get here, but 'here' isn't where I'm meant to be."

To my relief, he rallied behind me. His support gave me the final push I needed.

The next few weeks were a whirlwind. Telling my boss, my team, my colleagues— each conversation was difficult in its own way. Some were supportive, others were clearly disappointed. A few thought I was having a mid-life crisis. "You're joking, right?" one colleague asked incredulously, gesturing at the opulent office around us. "I know this is a joke and tomorrow you will say you were just joking."

His words stung, but they also reinforced my decision. Yes, I was walking away from "all this", the prestige, the comfort, the certainty. But I was walking to-wards something far more valuable: the chance to build something of my own, to pursue a vision that truly excited me.

As I stood on that balcony in Sentosa, overlooking the pristine beaches and luxurious yachts, I realized that I had achieved everything society told me I should want. And yet, I felt trapped. This moment of clarity forced me to confront a truth that many aspiring entrepreneurs face: the allure and danger of the comfort trap.

Rule: Break Free from the Comfort Trap

The traditional route—whether in your career, relationships, or personal life—offers predictability, but at a significant cost. While it may provide a sense of security, it often stifles innovation and prevents people from truly understanding what they're capable of. It wasn't until I decided to leave my corporate job and start my own business that I realized how much of my potential had been lying dormant. I had been following the "rules," doing what was expected of me, but I wasn't thriving. I was merely existing.

Understanding the Comfort Trap

The comfort trap is a psychological phenomenon that keeps us stuck in situations that are familiar and safe, even when they no longer serve our growth or happiness. It's the voice that whispers, "Why risk what you have for an uncertain future?" It's the force that makes us cling to our current circumstances, even when we know deep down that we're capable of so much more.

In my case, the comfort trap manifested as a prestigious job title, a generous salary, and a coveted address. On paper, I had it all. But these trappings of success had become a gilded cage, constraining my potential and stifling my entrepreneurial spirit.

The Illusion of Security

One of the most potent aspects of the comfort trap is the illusion of security it provides. Conventional wisdom tells us that if we follow a certain path—get a good education, climb the corporate ladder, save for retirement—we'll be safe and successful. But in today's rapidly changing world, is any path truly "safe?"

The security offered by traditional career paths is often more illusory than real. Companies downsize, industries become obsolete, and economic shifts can render once-stable jobs precarious. By clinging to this false sense of security, we may actually put ourselves at greater risk by not developing the adaptability and resilience that entrepreneurship fosters.

The Hidden Costs of Comfort

When we're caught in the comfort trap, we often overlook the hidden costs of our choices. Every time we choose the conventional path over the road less traveled, we're potentially missing out on extraordinary opportunities for growth, learning, and success.

In my journey, the cost of staying in my banking career would have been the loss of personal growth, the thrill of building something from scratch, and the deep satisfaction of pursuing my genuine passions. It would have meant never knowing what I could truly achieve.

Moreover, there's an emotional and psychological cost to staying in a situation that doesn't align with our deepest values and aspirations. It can lead to a sense of stagnation, unfulfillment, and even depression. The comfort trap may keep us "safe," but it often does so at the expense of our happiness and sense of purpose.

Breaking Free: The First Step Towards Entrepreneurship

Recognizing that you're caught in the comfort trap is the first step towards breaking free. For me, this realization came during a lunch with colleagues when I felt like an impostor in my own successful career. It was a jarring moment, but also a liberating one.

Breaking free from the comfort trap doesn't mean you have to immediately quit your job and start a business. It starts with small steps:

- **Ask the Tough Questions**: Take time to assess your current situation. Are you truly fulfilled, or just comfortable?

- **Identify Your Passions**: What excites you? What would you do if fear wasn't holding you back?

- **Set Small, Challenging Goals**: Start pushing your boundaries in small ways. This could be learning a new skill, networking outside your usual circles, or starting a side project.

- **Embrace Discomfort**: Recognize that growth and comfort rarely coexist. Start seeing discomfort as a sign of progress rather than something to be avoided.

- **Visualize Your Potential**: Imagine where you could be in five or ten years if you weren't constrained by your current circumstances. Let this vision pull you forward.

The Expat Advantage: Using Distance to Break the Trap

As an expat, you're in a unique position to break free from the comfort trap. Moving to a new country already requires stepping out of your comfort zone in numerous ways. You've had to adapt to a new culture, possibly learn a new language, and build a new network from scratch. In many ways, you've already rejected conventional wisdom by choosing to live abroad.

This experience of adapting to life in a foreign country can be a powerful tool in breaking free from the comfort trap in your professional life. You've already proven to yourself that you can thrive in unfamiliar and challenging circumstances. Why not apply that same courage and adaptability to your career?

Embracing Discomfort as a Catalyst for Growth

The irony of the comfort trap is that true comfort—the kind that comes from living an authentic, fulfilling life—often lies on the other side of discomfort. As an entrepreneur, especially as an expat entrepreneur, you'll face numerous challenges and uncertainties. But it's precisely these challenges that will push you to grow, innovate, and ultimately succeed.

Starting my own business forced me to confront all the ways I had been playing it safe. There was no roadmap, no instruction manual for how to build a successful business, especially as an expat in a foreign country. And while that lack of structure felt overwhelming at times, it also gave me the freedom to create my own path.

This freedom to innovate, to make mistakes and learn from them, to shape your own destiny—this sets successful entrepreneurs apart. By breaking free from the comfort trap, we open ourselves up to new possibilities and ways of thinking that can lead to revolutionary ideas and approaches.

The Reward: Personal Fulfillment and Professional Success

Breaking free from the comfort trap isn't easy. It requires courage, resilience, and a willingness to embrace uncertainty. But the rewards can be transformative.

In my own experience, it wasn't until I stepped away from my "successful" banking career that I felt truly alive. The challenges of entrepreneurship, while daunting, filled me with a sense of purpose and excitement that I had never experienced in my corporate role.

As an entrepreneur, you have the opportunity to create something meaningful, to solve problems that matter to you, and to shape your life and work in alignment with your values. You have the chance to discover what you're truly capable of, unfettered by the limitations of conventional career paths.

CASE STUDY: THE GOLDEN HANDCUFFS OF SUCCESS

Meet Jack, a 35-year-old management consultant from Austin, Texas. On paper, Jack's life is the epitome of success. He grew up in a middle-class family in Houston, where the expectations were clear: study hard, get into a good college, land a prestigious job, and climb the corporate ladder.

Jack followed this path to the letter. He graduated with honors from the University of Texas at Austin with a degree in Business Administration. Upon graduation, he landed a coveted position at a top consulting firm in Dallas. Over the next decade, Jack's career flourished. He consistently exceeded his targets, earned glowing performance reviews, and steadily climbed the ranks.

By his early thirties, Jack had it all—or so it seemed. He was now a senior manager at his firm, commanding a six-figure salary. He owned a sleek condo in a trendy Austin neighborhood, drove a luxury car, and took lavish vacations. His parents beamed with pride, and his peers looked at him with a mixture of admiration and envy.

But despite all the trappings of success, Jack felt... empty.

At first, Jack couldn't understand why he felt this way. He did everything by the book. He finally had the career, salary, and life he'd been told would be fulfilling—but was it? It was one of the most financially comfortable eras in his life. And yet, that comfort felt more like a cage than a sanctuary.

Jack daydreamed about starting his own business. He had ideas—innovative solutions to problems he'd encountered in his consulting work. But every time he considered taking the leap, the voice of conventional wisdom held him back:

"Why risk everything when you're doing so well?" "You'd be crazy to give up this security." "What if you fail? You'll never get a job like this again."

These thoughts kept Jack firmly in his comfort zone, but they also kept him from pursuing his true passions and potential.

The turning point came during a routine client meeting. Jack was presenting a strategy that he knew would boost the client's profits, but he also knew it would lead to significant layoffs. As he watched the executives nod approvingly at his slides, Jack felt a wave of disillusionment wash over him. Is this really what he wanted to do with his life? Make the rich richer at the expense of ordinary workers?

That night, Jack couldn't sleep. He realized he had been caught in the comfort trap. He had been so focused on achieving the next promotion, the next pay raise, that he had lost sight of what truly mattered to him. His job provided financial security and social status, but it didn't align with his values or fulfill his desire to make a meaningful impact.

Jack also recognized the hidden costs of his comfortable life. He had stopped learning and growing, content to rely on his existing skills rather than pushing himself to develop new ones. His network was limited to other consultants and clients, all operating within the same corporate mindset. He had ideas for innovative business solutions, but he had never taken the risk of developing them.

The next day, Jack took the first small step out of his comfort zone. He signed up for a local entrepreneurship meetup, something he had always been curious about but had never made time for. At the meetup, he met people who had taken the leap from corporate jobs to start their own businesses. Their stories of challenges and triumphs resonated deeply with Jack.

Over the next few months, Jack gradually began to expand his comfort zone. He started dedicating his weekends to developing one of his business ideas. He took online courses in areas outside his expertise. He even had conversations with his boss about reducing his hours to pursue some personal projects.

It wasn't easy. There were moments of doubt, fear, and the temptation to retreat to the safety of his familiar routine. But with each small step outside his comfort zone, Jack felt more alive, more aligned with his true self.

A year later, Jack made the leap. He left his consulting job to start his own business—a platform that helped companies implement ethical AI solutions. The journey was challenging, filled with ups and downs, moments of exhilaration, and moments of doubt. But even on the toughest days, Jack never felt the emptiness that had plagued him in his corporate job.

Four Key Lessons from Jack's Comfort Trap Escape

1. **Recognize the Illusion of Security**: Jack's journey illustrates how traditional career paths, while seemingly secure, can often lead to stagnation and unfulfillment. True security comes from developing adaptable skills and pursuing meaningful work, not from clinging to a comfortable but unsatisfying status quo.

2. **Align Actions with Values**: Jack's discomfort in his consulting role stemmed from a misalignment between his work and his personal values. His decision to start an ethical AI company demonstrates the importance of pursuing ventures that resonate with your core beliefs and desires.

3. **Embrace Incremental Change**: Jack didn't quit his job immediately. Instead, he took small steps like attending entrepreneurship meetups and developing his business idea on weekends. This gradual approach to change can make the transition out of the comfort zone less daunting and more sustainable.

4. **Reframe Risk and Reward**: Initially, Jack saw leaving his job as a risk. However, he came to realize that staying in an unfulfilling career was the bigger risk—a risk to his personal growth, happiness, and potential. This shift in perspective allowed him to see entrepreneurship not as a danger, but as an opportunity for fulfillment and impact.

These lessons from Jack's story highlight the transformative power of breaking free from the comfort trap. By recognizing the limitations of conventional paths, aligning our actions with our values, embracing gradual change, and reframing our perception of risk, we can escape the golden handcuffs of success and pursue more meaningful and fulfilling endeavors.

Take a Moment to Reflect

Jack's story illustrates the subtle yet powerful grip of the comfort trap, and the transformative potential of breaking free. While not everyone's path will lead to starting a business, Jack's journey highlights universal truths about comfort, growth, and fulfillment. Let's explore how you can apply these insights to your own life and career.

Reflection Questions:

1. In what ways can you relate to Jack's initial situation? Are there areas in your life where external success might mask internal dissatisfaction?

2. What dreams or ideas have you been putting off in favor of security and comfort?

3. Can you identify any "golden handcuffs" in your own life—things that keep you comfortable but might hold you back from greater fulfillment?

4. How has your comfort zone expanded or contracted over the past few years? What impact has this had on your personal and professional growth?

5. What would your life look like two years from now if, like Jack, you pursued your entrepreneurial dreams?

Take Action:

- **Conduct a Comfort Audit**: Take a week to observe and note down moments when you choose comfort over growth. This could be as simple as taking the same route to work every day or avoiding a challenging conversation. Awareness is the first step to change.

- **The Daily Discomfort Challenge**: Choose one small action each day that jogs you out of your comfort zone. This could strike up a conversation with a stranger, trying a new food, or learning a new skill for fifteen minutes.

- **Skill Expansion Project**: Identify a skill that would be useful for your entrepreneurial goals but that you've been avoiding learning. Commit to spending 30 minutes twice a week for a month on developing this skill.

- **The Alternative Path Visualization**: Spend 10 minutes each day for a week visualizing your life five years from now if you pursue your entrepreneurial dreams. Be as detailed as possible. Then spend ten minutes visualizing your life if you stay in your current comfort zone.

- **Network Expansion Challenge**: Attend one networking event or reach out to one person in your industry (or desired industry) each month. This could be as simple as a coffee meetup or a LinkedIn connection.

- **The Micro-Entrepreneurship Experiment**: Start a small side project or freelance gig related to your entrepreneurial interests. This could be as simple as selling a handmade item online or offering a service on a freelance platform.

- **The Comfort Zone Journal**: Keep a journal for a month where you document one instance each day where you stepped out of your comfort zone, no matter how small. Note what you learned or gained from each experience.

- **The Failure Reframe**: The next time you experience a setback or "failure," practice reframing it as a learning opportunity. Write down three things you learned from the experience and how you can apply these lessons.

By engaging with these reflections and actions, you'll expand your comfort zone and build the resilience necessary for entrepreneurial success. Remember, the goal isn't to eliminate comfort entirely, but to become comfortable with discomfort—a key trait of successful entrepreneurs.

Your Invitation to Break Free

The comfort trap is a powerful force, but it's not insurmountable. By recognizing its allure and understanding its limitations, you've already taken the first step towards breaking free.

As you continue reading this book and exploring your entrepreneurial journey, I encourage you to keep pushing against the boundaries of your comfort zone. Embrace the discomfort that comes with growth and change. Remember, on the other side of that discomfort lies a world of possibility—a world where you can thrive, not just exist.

In the next chapter, we'll explore strategies for building the confidence and resilience necessary to not just break free from the comfort trap, but to flourish in the exciting and challenging world of entrepreneurship.

CHAPTER 3

Reclaim Your Identity

"To be yourself in a world that is constantly trying to make you something else is the greatest accomplishment."

–Ralph Waldo Emerson

Why do our clothes make up so much of our identity? What is it about what we wear that seems to define us, both to ourselves and to others? And why does shedding that familiar attire feel like shedding a part of ourselves?

These questions swirled in my mind as I stood in front of my closet, my crisp button-down white shirt feeling like a straitjacket. My fingers hovered over the familiar row of dark suits, hesitating. Today was different. I wasn't heading to a corporate office or a client meeting. I was stepping into my role as an entrepreneur, a content creator, and a podcaster. Yet the weight of my 15-year legal career hung heavy on my shoulders.

For over a decade, I had worn the uniform of corporate success—dark suits, white shirts, and black heels. It wasn't just clothing; it was armor. It signaled competence, reliability, and conformity to the unwritten rules of the legal world. As a lawyer, I had learned to modulate my speech, to weigh every word, and to present a polished, professional image at all times. I had perfected a persona that had served me well in boardrooms and social settings alike.

But now, as an entrepreneur, that armor felt suffocating.

I reached past the suits, my hand trembling slightly as I grabbed a colorful button-down shirt. It felt like an act of rebellion. As I put it on, I caught sight of myself in the mirror. The person staring back at me looked more like... me. Not the corporate lawyer, not the Global Head of Data Privacy, but just... me.

Yet with that authenticity came a wave of anxiety. What would my former colleagues think if they saw me like this? Would potential clients still take me seriously? The questions that had plagued me for months came flooding back.

I picked up my phone, opening Instagram to post about a new podcast episode. My finger hovered over the 'Share' button. Despite two years of entrepreneurship, this simple act filled me with dread. The content was good, I knew that. But putting myself out there, showing the world this new version of me—it felt like stepping off a cliff.

I thought back to my carefully curated LinkedIn profile. It told the story of a successful international lawyer, showcasing awards, speaking engagements, and career milestones. It was impressive, polished, and entirely at odds with the person I was becoming—the person I wanted to be.

The dichotomy was stark. On one platform, I was the serious, corporate lawyer. On others, I was exploring new ideas, creating content, and sharing insights that went beyond the realm of legal expertise. The gap between these personas felt like a chasm, and I was straddling it precariously.

I closed my eyes, took a deep breath, and pressed 'Share'. The anxiety didn't disappear, but alongside it, I felt a glimmer of something else—liberation.

As I made my way to a coffee shop to work on my latest project, I couldn't help but notice the looks I was getting. Was it just my imagination, or were people seeing me differently? I felt exposed, vulnerable. The protective layer of my corporate identity was gone, and I felt naked without it.

Sitting down with my laptop, I opened my email to find a message from a former colleague. "Saw your latest TikTok," it read. "Interesting career shift. Are you still practicing law?"

My heart raced. This was exactly what I had feared—judgment, questioning, doubt. The urge to defend myself, to remind them of my legal credentials, was overwhelming. But as I started to type out a response, I paused.

Why was I so afraid of what others thought? Why did I feel the need to justify my choices? The realization hit me like a tidal wave—I had spent so long conforming to others' expectations that I had lost sight of my own desires, my own path.

At that moment, I made a decision. I deleted the defensive response I had been drafting and instead wrote: "Thanks for reaching out. Yes, it's been an exciting journey. I'd love to tell you more about it sometime."

It was a small step, but it felt monumental. For the first time, I wasn't apologizing for my choices or hiding behind my legal persona. I was embracing my new path, acknowledging that it was different and being okay with that.

As I closed my laptop, I felt a weight lift off my shoulders. The fear of judgment was still there, a constant companion on this entrepreneurial journey. But now, instead of letting it paralyze me, I recognized it for what it was—a sign that I was growing, evolving, stepping into a new version of myself.

The path ahead was still uncertain. I knew there would be more moments of doubt, more instances where I'd question whether I was doing the right thing. But I also knew that the only way forward was through—through the discomfort, through the fear, through the judgment.

As I walked out of the coffee shop, the sun warm on my face, I realized something profound. The real challenge wasn't in starting a business or creating content.

The real challenge was in fully embracing who I was becoming, in allowing myself to be seen—truly seen—for the first time in years.

The lawyer's armor was shed, and beneath it, an entrepreneur was emerging. It was scary, exhilarating, and absolutely necessary. Because at the end of the day, the fear of judgment paled compared to the fear of never fully becoming who I was meant to be. As we navigate the entrepreneurial journey, particularly as expats, one of the most formidable obstacles we face is not external, but internal: the fear of judgment. This fear can be paralyzing, keeping us tethered to familiar paths and preventing us from fully embracing our true potential. In this chapter, we'll explore how the RISE Method can help you overcome this fear and step into your authentic self.

Rule: The RISE Method: Reclaiming Identity, Strengthening Essence

As we navigate the entrepreneurial journey, particularly as expats, one of the most formidable obstacles we face is not external, but internal: the fear of judgment. This fear can be paralyzing, keeping us tethered to familiar paths and preventing us from fully embracing our true potential. The RISE Method provides a framework for overcoming this fear and stepping into our authentic selves.

R—Recognize Your Professional Identity's Weight

Our professional identities often become more than just job titles; they evolve into integral parts of how we see ourselves and how others perceive us. This identity can provide a sense of security, belonging, and status. It's the lawyer's crisp suit, the doctor's white coat, the executive's corner office—symbols that speak volumes before we even open our mouths.

However, this professional identity can also become a cage, limiting our ability to grow and change. It can create expectations—both from others and ourselves—about how we should behave, what we should value, and what success looks like. When we consider stepping outside these expectations, we often face a deep-seated fear of disappointing others or losing our hard-earned status.

Recognizing the weight of our professional identity is crucial. It involves understanding:

- How much of our self-worth is tied to our job title
- How our career shapes our decision-making
- How it influences our relationships

Only by acknowledging this weight can we discern between who we are and what we do for a living.

I—Integrate Your Evolving Self

As we evolve in our personal and professional lives, we often find a growing disparity between who we are and who we're becoming. This 'identity gap' can manifest in various ways:

- Maintaining different personas on different social media platforms
- Feeling like an impostor in new roles or environments
- Struggling to introduce ourselves without relying on our old job title
- Hesitating to share new interests or pursuits with old colleagues or friends

This gap can create internal turmoil, making us feel inauthentic or divided. We might find ourselves code-switching between our 'professional' self and our 'real' self, unsure of how to reconcile the two.

Integrating our evolving self involves:

- Honoring our professional background while embracing new aspects of ourselves
- Gradually introducing new elements of our personality into our professional life

- Finding creative ways to apply our professional skills to new pursuits

S—Shift to Internal Validation

Many of us have been conditioned to seek approval and validation from external sources—colleagues, bosses, clients, or society at large. This external focus can keep us trapped in roles that no longer serve us, making decisions based on others' expectations rather than on our own desires and values.

Shifting from external to internal validation is a transformative process. It involves:

- Recognizing the sources of our desire for approval

- Learning to trust our own judgment and intuition

- Defining success on our own terms, rather than societal standards

- Developing the courage to make choices that align with our values, even if they're not understood or appreciated by others

This shift doesn't mean disregarding others' opinions entirely, but giving primacy to our own sense of purpose and fulfillment. It's about building a strong internal compass that can guide us through the inevitable doubts and challenges of entrepreneurial life.

E—Embrace Personal Evolution

Change is the only constant in life, yet it's something many of us resist, especially when it comes to our own identities. We often cling to outdated self-images, fearing that change might mean a loss of who we are.

Embracing personal evolution involves:

- Accepting that growth often requires leaving behind old versions of ourselves

- Being open to new experiences and perspectives that challenge our existing beliefs

- Allowing our definition of success to evolve as we gain new insights and priorities
- Seeing setbacks and failures as opportunities for learning and redefinition

This component is about more than just accepting change—it's about actively pursuing growth and new definitions of success. It's recognizing that our identity is not fixed, but fluid, constantly being shaped by our experiences and choices.

Embracing evolution also means extending the same acceptance to others in our lives. As we change, our relationships may need to evolve too. Some may grow stronger as we become more authentic, while others may naturally drift apart.

In the following case study, we'll see how these themes play out in real life, exploring the journey of an individual who grappled with and ultimately overcame the fear of judgment to embrace a more authentic path. As you read, reflect on how these themes resonate with your own experiences and aspirations.

CASE STUDY: SARAH'S JOURNEY—THE RISE METHOD IN ACTION

Sarah Thompson, 37, had spent the last decade climbing the corporate ladder at GlobeTech, a multinational tech company. As the Senior Vice President of Human Resources, she oversaw HR policies and practices for over 10,000 employees across three continents. Sarah was the epitome of corporate success—polished, professional, and perpetually composed.

Her role demanded a certain image. Every day, Sarah donned her armor: a crisp blazer, a silk blouse, and heels that clicked authoritatively down the hallways of GlobeTech's gleaming headquarters. She was looked up to by hundreds of employees, seen as a paragon of professionalism and corporate values.

GlobeTech had strict policies about employees' online presence, particularly for executives. As the enforcer of these policies, Sarah was hyper-aware of maintaining a squeaky-clean online image. Her LinkedIn profile was a testament to corporate achievement, but beyond that, Sarah was a ghost in the digital world. No Twitter, no Instagram, no personal blog–nothing that might reflect who she was as a person.

However, after years of helping others navigate their careers, Sarah felt a growing disconnect between her corporate persona and her true self. She yearned to make a broader impact, to help companies create more human-centric workplaces. The idea of starting her own HR consultancy took root.

But when Sarah finally left GlobeTech and start her own business, she found herself paralyzed with fear. How could she present herself to the world after years of carefully curated anonymity? The thought of putting herself out there–of being seen, judged, potentially criticized–was terrifying.

Sarah's journey to overcome this fear and embrace her authentic self was not a straight path. She realized how much of her self-worth was tied to her corporate title and the respect it commanded. She had to confront the uncomfortable truth that without her SVP title, she felt vulnerable and unsure of her value.

Sarah struggled to reconcile the polished corporate executive she had been with the more approachable, relatable consultant she wanted to become. She hired a fashion consultant to help her develop a personal style that felt both professional and authentic, ditching the conservative suits for outfits that expressed more of her personality.

Years of seeking approval from higher-ups and being responsible for others' careers had left Sarah overly concerned with others' opinions. She started therapy to work through her fear of judgment and learn to trust her own instincts. Her therapist introduced her to mindfulness practices, which Sarah incorporated into her daily routine.

Sarah began journaling daily, exploring who she was beyond her corporate role. She rediscovered passions she had set aside years ago—her love for modern art, her interest in sustainable living. She saw how these personal interests could inform and enrich her approach to HR consulting.

The turning point came when Sarah was invited to speak at a small HR conference. Initially, she prepared a safe, corporate-style presentation. But the night before, inspired by a particularly insightful therapy session, she rewrote the entire thing.

The next day, Sarah stepped on stage, not in a suit, but in a vibrant dress that made her feel confident and alive. She spoke not just about HR best practices, but about her personal journey and her vision for more human-centric workplaces. Her authenticity resonated deeply with the audience.

After the conference, Sarah was approached by several potential clients who connected with her message and her genuine approach. She realized that by being her true self, she was attracting the kind of clients she truly wanted to work with.

This experience gave Sarah the confidence to fully embrace her new identity as an entrepreneur. She launched a website that showcased not just her professional expertise, but also her personality and values. She started a blog sharing her thoughts on HR trends, peppered with personal anecdotes and lessons from her own career.

Sarah's journey wasn't without setbacks. Some former colleagues criticized her new approach, calling it "unprofessional." There were moments of doubt when client leads didn't pan out. But Sarah had learned to validate herself internally. She stayed true to her authentic self, and gradually, her consultancy thrived.

Two years into her entrepreneurial journey, Sarah's business was flourishing. She had built a reputation not just for her HR expertise, but for her authentic, human-centric approach. Sarah realized that the very things she had feared would repel clients—her personality, her unconventional ideas, her openness about her own journey—were precisely what attracted them.

Key Points from Sarah's Journey: The RISE Method in Action

Recognize Your Professional Identity's Weight:

- Sarah realized how deeply her self-worth was tied to her SVP title at GlobeTech

- She understood that her corporate role had created a false sense of security

- Acknowledging this dependence on her professional identity was crucial for Sarah's growth

Integrate Your Evolving Self:

- Sarah worked with a fashion consultant to bridge the gap between her corporate and entrepreneurial identities

- She incorporated her passion for modern art and sustainable living into her HR consulting approach

- Sarah's new identity blended her past corporate experience with her authentic personality

Shift to Internal Validation:

- Sarah recognized how much she had relied on approval from higher-ups and colleagues

- She engaged in therapy, mindfulness practices, and daily journaling to build self-trust

- Sarah redefined success based on personal fulfillment rather than external metrics

Embrace Personal Evolution:

- Sarah's authentic presentation at the HR conference led to unexpected client opportunities

- Her genuine approach became a key attractor for the clients she truly wanted to work with

- Despite setbacks, Sarah committed to ongoing personal growth and authenticity in her business

Sarah's story illustrates the profound transformation that can occur when we confront our fear of judgment and embrace our authentic selves. By recognizing the weight of her professional identity, integrating her evolving self, shifting to internal validation, and embracing her personal evolution, Sarah could create a new career that aligned with her true self, and ironically, achieve even greater success than before.

Take a Moment to Reflect

The RISE Method helps you reconnect with your authentic self beyond your professional identity. By following these steps and reflecting deeply, you can achieve a more balanced and fulfilling life that integrates all aspects of who you are.

Reflection Questions:

1. How much of your self-worth is tied to your professional identity?

2. What aspects of your personality do you feel you've suppressed in your professional life?

3. What does success look like to you, independent of others' expectations?

4. What old self-image are you holding onto that might be limiting your growth?

These questions encourage deep introspection about your identity, values, and personal growth. Take your time with each question, allowing yourself to explore your thoughts and feelings fully. Remember, the RISE Method is an ongoing process. Regularly revisiting these actions and reflections can help you continue to grow and align your life *Action Steps:*

1. List your professional achievements, titles, and responsibilities. Reflect on how each makes you feel about yourself.

2. Identify three personal interests or passions you've neglected due to work. Brainstorm ways to incorporate them into your professional life.

3. Start a daily journaling practice, focusing on your personal values and what success means to you.

4. Identify a skill or area of knowledge outside your current expertise that you'd like to develop.

Implement these actions in your daily life. They will help you reconnect with your authentic self and broaden your self-perception beyond your professional role.

Overcoming Fear of Judgment with the RISE Method

In this chapter, we've explored one of the most significant internal obstacles faced by expat entrepreneurs: the fear of judgment. Through a personal narrative and introducing the RISE Method, we've uncovered strategies to overcome this fear and embrace our authentic selves in our professional lives.

We began with a vivid account of the internal struggle many face when transitioning from a traditional corporate role to entrepreneurship. The story of shedding the "armor" of corporate attire and persona resonated with the deeper challenge of letting go of a carefully cultivated professional identity. This narrative highlighted the anxiety, vulnerability, and ultimately, the liberation that comes with embracing one's authentic self in a professional context.

The core of our discussion centered on the RISE Method, a framework designed to help individuals reclaim their identity and strengthen their essence:

1. **Recognize Your Professional Identity's Weight**: We examined how our job titles and roles can become integral to our self-perception, often limiting our ability to grow and change.

2. **Integrate Your Evolving Self**: We discussed strategies for bridging the gap between our professional persona and our authentic selves, bringing more of our true personality into our work.

3. **Shift to Internal Validation**: We explored the importance of moving away from external sources of approval and learning to trust our own judgment and intuition.

4. **Embrace Personal Evolution**: We emphasized the need to see change not as a threat to our identity, but as an opportunity for growth and self-discovery.

The case study of Sarah brought these concepts to life, illustrating how the RISE Method can help overcome the fear of judgment and create a more authentic, fulfilling professional life. Sarah's journey from a corporate executive to a successful entrepreneur showed the challenges and rewards of this process.

As we conclude this chapter, it's clear that overcoming the fear of judgment is not just about professional success–it's about personal fulfillment and living an authentic life. The RISE Method provides a roadmap for this journey, but it's important to remember that this is an ongoing process, not a one-time transformation.

For expat entrepreneurs, this journey can be challenging and rewarding. Your experiences across different cultures and environments have likely already pushed you to adapt and grow. You can use these same skills to shape your professional identity in a way that aligns with your true self.

Remember, the fear of judgment is often rooted in the belief that we must conform to others' expectations to be successful. However, as we've seen through the examples in this chapter, genuine success often comes when we have the courage to be authentic. Your unique perspectives, experiences, and personality are not liabilities to be hidden, but assets to be leveraged.

As you move forward in your entrepreneurial journey, challenge yourself to apply the RISE Method in your daily life. Recognize the weight of your professional identity, but don't let it define you. Integrate new aspects of yourself into your work. Shift your focus to internal validation, trusting your own judgment. And most importantly, embrace your personal evolution, seeing each change as an opportunity for growth.

By doing so, you're not just building a business–you're crafting a professional life that reflects your true self. This authenticity will not only lead to greater personal satisfaction but can also become your unique selling point in the marketplace. In a world that often values conformity, your authentic self can be your greatest differentiator.

The path to authenticity may not always be easy. There will be moments of doubt, fear, and discomfort. But remember, on the other side of this fear lies the opportunity to fully become who you are meant to be. And that, ultimately, is the greatest success of all.

CHAPTER 4

Family as Your Superpower

"You don't have to choose between your career and your family. You can have both if you're willing to work for it."

–Sheryl Sandberg

The humid Singapore air hung heavy as I stood in the kitchen, packing lunches for the boys. Liam, my ten-year-old, was chattering about a school project while Leland, his eight-year-old brother, scrambled to find his favorite shoes. Mornings were always a blur—getting the boys ready for school while my mind was already racing toward the workday ahead.

"Mom, are you going on another trip?" Liam asked, his wide eyes full of curiosity and a bit of worry.

I paused, catching his gaze. "Not today," I said, smiling gently. "But next week I have to go to Hong Kong for a few days, just for work."

Liam's face dropped slightly. "How many days this time?"

"Just three," I reassured him, though I could feel the familiar guilt creeping in. "I'll be back before the weekend, I promise."

Leland, standing beside him, looked up from tying his shoes. "But you were gone last week, Mom. Why do you have to go again?"

"I know," I said, feeling the weight of their questions. "It's part of my job. We'll FaceTime every night, just like I always do."

They both nodded, but their eyes held the questions they didn't know how to ask yet. This was my reality back then—twice a month, I would pack my bags for international business trips. As Vice President of Legal and Compliance for Marriott International, covering the Asia-Pacific, I spent a lot of time in airports, on planes, and in unfamiliar destinations—Indonesia, Australia, India, Hong Kong. Every trip meant being away from my boys for days at a time, and every goodbye felt harder than the last.

As soon as I boarded a flight to Bangkok or Tokyo, my mind would shift gears. It was all business—meetings, training, and investigations. I'd call home every night, but sometimes I missed the boys before they went to bed. The guilt would hit me hard during those long flights home, knowing I'd missed their soccer games, their homework struggles, their stories from school. I felt torn between my role as a mother and the demands of my career.

But when I transitioned into being a founder, I thought things would change. No more monthly flights, no more time away from home. I imagined having more time with Liam and Leland, more time to be present. Instead, I found myself working twice as hard—only now, I was doing it from the kitchen table. My laptop became a permanent fixture in the living room, and I was constantly checking emails and drafting proposals, even while the boys were playing nearby.

One evening, as I typed furiously on my laptop while the boys ate dinner, Leland tugged at my sleeve. "Mom, are you working again?"

I glanced up, caught off guard. "Just finishing something, sweetie. I'll be done soon."

"But you said that yesterday," Liam chimed in, his voice soft but serious. "You're here, but you're not really here."

Their words cut deeper than I expected. I was home, but I wasn't present. I'd left behind the constant travel, but now work followed me everywhere. It was time to make a change.

That night, after the boys went to bed, I sat down with my husband, and we talked about how things needed to shift. "I can't keep doing this," I admitted. "I'm home, but I'm not *really* with them. I need to find a way to make this work."

"Let's figure out a better schedule," he suggested. "You can work hard, but you've got to carve out time for the kids."

The first thing I did was organize my life with Google Calendar. I created blocks of time—green for family, blue for work, and red for self-care. I made sure that from 4 PM to 8 PM every day, I was fully present with Liam and Leland. No emails, no phone calls, no work.

"Boys," I announced at dinner the next day, "from now on, I'm all yours after six o'clock. No work. Just family time."

Leland grinned widely. "Does that mean we can play soccer in the park?"

"Absolutely," I said, smiling back. "Whatever you guys want."

Liam, more reserved, gave a small nod. "Can we still help you with work sometimes? I like hearing about your projects."

It was then that I realized I didn't have to separate work and family completely. I could involve them in age-appropriate ways. "Of course! You can help me brainstorm ideas or organize things. We can work on fun stuff together."

And we did. I began explaining parts of my business to them, showing them how I made TikTok and YouTube videos. I even let them help with simple tasks like organizing my workspace or coming up with creative ideas. They loved it. It became a way for us to connect, and it shifted their perception of my work from something that took me away to something we could share.

The next practical step I took was setting clear boundaries. I told my clients that after 8 PM, I wouldn't be available until the next morning. I set my phone to "Do Not Disturb" during family time and made sure that work stayed in its designated time blocks. It wasn't easy at first—there were always emails waiting, always something that seemed urgent. But over time, I learned to trust that the world wouldn't fall apart if I didn't respond immediately.

The guilt that had weighed on me for years lifted. I wasn't trying to be everything to everyone all at once anymore. I was making intentional choices—balancing work and family in a way that allowed me to be present for both. And my kids noticed the difference. By creating boundaries, involving my boys in my work, and setting intentional time for both family and business, I found a balance that worked for all of us.

Rule: Balance Without Guilt

As an entrepreneur raising children while building a business abroad, it can be incredibly challenging to find a balance between your responsibilities as a parent and the demands of your business. The key is to strive for balance without guilt—acknowledging that while both your children and your business need your time, it's possible to create moments where they coexist harmoniously.

One of the biggest mistakes many people make when building a business is neglecting their family in favor of growth. It's important to recognize that your children, whether they live with you or are in a different country, are a crucial part of your "why." They are the reason you are striving to build something that provides stability, freedom, and opportunities for your family. The challenge lies in balancing your desire to succeed as an entrepreneur with your desire to be present as a parent.

Joint Activities That Blend Business and Family Time

One effective strategy is to find activities that allow you to do both—work on your business while spending quality time with your children. For example, you might:

- **Work at Family-Friendly Locations**: If you live in the same country as your children, consider working at locations where they can play or engage in activities while you focus on business tasks. Many hotels have kids' clubs or play areas, which allows you to spend some time working while they enjoy supervised activities. You can then join them afterward, making it a productive yet connected experience for both of you.

- **Involve Your Kids in Age-Appropriate Tasks**: Depending on their age, you can involve your children in your business in small ways. This can be a great bonding opportunity while also giving them a sense of what you do. Whether it's helping you pack products, setting up a workspace, or brainstorming creative ideas, involving your kids can be both fun and educational.

- **Create a Routine That Includes Both Work and Play**: Set specific times during the day when you dedicate yourself fully to your children and other times when you focus solely on work. This routine can help manage expectations for both you and your children, reducing feelings of guilt and ensuring that both aspects of your life receive the attention they need.

If Your Children Are in a Different Country

For those whose children are not currently living in the same country, the balance can feel even more challenging. In this situation, it's important to stay connected and let your children know they are the driving force behind your efforts. Here are some strategies to maintain that connection:

- **Schedule Regular Virtual Time Together**: Set aside dedicated time each week for video calls with your children. This helps maintain your bond and keeps them involved in your life, even from afar. Use this time to share your progress with them, letting them know that your hard work is all about creating a better future for your family.

- **Share Your Journey**: Make your children a part of your entrepreneurial journey by sharing stories and updates with them. Let them see how your work is progressing and why it matters. This helps them understand why you are working so hard and reinforces that your ultimate goal is to be reunited with them.

- **Plan Visits and Future Reunions**: When your children live in a different country, having something to look forward to can make all the difference. Plan regular visits or special trips together and use these reunions as motivation to keep pushing forward. The goal of being together again can provide the emotional drive you need to keep building your business.

Your Bigger Why

Ultimately, whether your children live with you or in another country, they are your "why"—the reason you're working so hard to build a successful business. Entrepreneurship is often about creating a better life, and for many parents, that means more time, freedom, and opportunities for their children. It's important to keep this "why" front and center, especially during challenging times.

Yes, there will be moments when you feel guilty—guilty for working when you could be with your children, or guilty for taking a break when there's work to be done. But remember, building a business is also about showing your children what's possible. It's about demonstrating resilience, ambition, and the courage to follow your dreams. By balancing your responsibilities thoughtfully and creatively, you can set an example that inspires your children to pursue their own passions.

Your journey is unique, and so is your approach to balancing family and entrepreneurship. Use the strategies that work for you, stay true to your values, and remember that you're doing this not just for yourself, but for your family's future.

As we explore the rule of *Balance Without Guilt*, it's essential to understand how this concept plays out in real life, especially for entrepreneurs raising children while pursuing their dreams abroad. One story that captures this balance comes from Kofi, a young man from Ghana who moved to Dubai to chase a business dream while his family remained back home. His journey illustrates the emotional complexities of balancing ambition and fatherhood, and how he strives to build something greater for his family, even from afar.

FROM GHANA TO DUBAI:
A FATHER'S JOURNEY TO BUILD A LEGACY

The early morning sunlight filtered through the curtains of Kofi's small apartment, casting a soft golden glow across the room. He stretched, feeling the familiar pang in his chest as he checked his phone for messages. As expected, there were none yet—it was still too early in Ghana. He missed them, especially in quiet moments like this. The sound of his children's laughter, the smell of Ama's cooking filling their home, and the warmth of family life—it all seemed so far away.

Kofi sighed, running a hand over his face before pushing himself out of bed. Today was just another day at the office, but it also marked the beginning of something bigger. He had a meeting later that evening with a potential investor. If this went well, his dream of starting a business in Dubai could finally take shape. Kofi had been working on an import-export business idea that connected Dubai's booming market with Ghana's rich agricultural resources. The logistics of trading goods between the two countries had fascinated him for years, and now, with the right investment, he could turn that passion into reality.

Later that night, after the office had emptied out, Kofi sat at a local café, nervously glancing at his phone. He couldn't stop thinking about Ama and the kids. They were back in Ghana, and he hadn't seen them in over a year. The video calls helped, but they were no substitute for being there. He felt guilty sometimes—guilty for chasing this dream while Ama held down the fort back home, raising their children without him.

His phone buzzed, shaking him from his thoughts. It was a message from Ama. He opened it, smiling as he saw a photo of their two kids, Adjoa, and Kwame, grinning from ear to ear, holding up drawings they had made at school.

"Look at your children," Ama's message read, "Both little artists. They're missing you, Kofi. We all are."

Kofi stared at the picture, his heart swelling and breaking at the same time. He could practically hear Adjoa's giggle and see Kwame's serious little face as he concentrated on his drawings. He wanted to be there with them, to see these moments for himself. But that wasn't his reality, not right now.

He began typing a reply, his fingers lingering. "I miss you all, too. Tell them Baba is working hard for them. Soon, we'll all be together."

Before he could hit send, his phone rang. It was Ama.

"Kofi, are you busy?" she asked, her voice calm but filled with the tiredness he knew all too well.

"I'm just waiting for a meeting," he replied, leaning back in his chair and closing his eyes. Hearing her voice brought him a sense of calm he hadn't felt all day. "How are things at home?"

"We're okay. The kids were asking about you today. Adjoa wants to know when you'll be home to take her to the park, like you used to."

Kofi's throat tightened. He hadn't realized how much he missed those small moments until now. "Tell her soon," he said, his voice cracking slightly. "I'm working on something, Ama. If this goes well, maybe I can bring you all here. I just need a little more time."

Ama was silent for a moment, and Kofi could hear the soft hum of life in the background—a car passing, the faint sound of children's voices, the clink of dishes. It made his heart ache.

"I know you're doing your best, Kofi," Ama said softly. "I just want to make sure you're taking care of yourself, too. Don't burn out. We need you in one piece when this is all done."

Kofi smiled, though she couldn't see it. "I'll be fine, Ama. I'm doing this for us. For the kids."

"I know," she said, her voice gentle but firm. "But just remember, they need their father, not just the businessman. Don't forget who you're doing this for."

"I won't," Kofi whispered, swallowing the lump in his throat. "I promise."

They hung up, and Kofi sat for a moment, staring at his phone, lost in thought. The investor would be there any minute, and he needed to pull himself together. This was his shot. He couldn't let himself be distracted by the distance or the guilt.

A few minutes later, a well-dressed man walked into the café, scanning the room until his eyes landed on Kofi. He stood, shaking the man's hand with a firm grip, masking the nerves that churned in his stomach.

"Kofi, good to meet you," the investor said, his voice smooth and practiced. "I've heard good things about your idea. Let's talk."

The two men sat down, and Kofi launched into his pitch. He had spent months researching how to build an import-export business focused on bringing fresh produce from Ghana to the bustling markets of Dubai. Ghana had a wealth of agricultural products, particularly cocoa and shea butter, which were in high demand in the luxury markets of the UAE. But the logistics were complicated—he needed capital for shipping, storage, and compliance with the UAE's strict import regulations.

"I believe there's a tremendous opportunity here," Kofi said, his voice steady but filled with emotion. "Dubai is a hub for trade, and the demand for organic, ethically sourced goods is growing. Ghana can supply those products, but we need a reliable infrastructure to make it happen. With your investment, I can build that bridge."

The investor listened carefully, nodding occasionally. Kofi continued, detailing his plans for securing partnerships with local farmers in Ghana, setting up a distribution center in Dubai, and using his network to tap into high-end retailers. He had thought through every aspect of the business—from the shipping routes to potential market fluctuations—and now all he needed was the financial backing to bring it to life.

After an hour of discussion, the investor leaned back, nodding thoughtfully. "You've got potential, Kofi," he said. "But starting a business here isn't easy. It'll take time, and you'll need to be prepared for some tough decisions. Are you ready for that?"

Kofi hesitated for a moment, thinking of Ama's words. He thought of his kids, of their faces lighting up on the screen whenever they saw him, of the sacrifices they were all making for this dream. He had to make it work.

"I'm ready," Kofi said, his voice steady. "I'm doing this for my family."

The investor smiled. "Good. Then let's see where this goes."

As Kofi walked home that night, the city lights glittering around him, he felt a mixture of hope and fear. The road ahead was long, and he wasn't sure how everything would turn out. But one thing was certain—he was doing this for them, and that made it all worth it.

Kofi's story is one of sacrifice, ambition, and a deep desire to provide for his family, even though they are separated by distance. He is constantly navigating the challenges of entrepreneurship, while also staying connected to his wife and children in Ghana. Let's now explore the strategies he uses to keep that balance intact and how you can apply similar methods to your own entrepreneurial journey abroad.

How Kofi Applied the Balance Without Guilt Rule

Kofi's journey to build an import-export business in Dubai while his wife and children remained in Ghana is a powerful example of the *Balance Without Guilt* rule in action. His story illustrates how challenging it can be to pursue entrepreneurial dreams when your heart is split between building a future and staying present for your family. But Kofi honored both his business aspirations and his responsibilities as a father and husband, without letting guilt overshadow his efforts.

Maintaining Emotional Connection

Despite the physical distance, Kofi stayed emotionally connected to his family. Through regular video calls, photos, and messages, he kept the bond strong, reminding his children that they were at the center of his purpose. His connection to Ama, his wife, also played a critical role in his ability to navigate the guilt of being away. Instead of letting the guilt consume him, Kofi used these moments of connection to fuel his determination. He shared his dreams with his children, letting them know that his hard work was about building a better future for them.

Kofi found that by regularly sharing updates with his family, he could bridge the gap of distance. He wasn't just working for them—he was working *with* them, making them part of his entrepreneurial vision. This approach helped ease the guilt of missing key moments and strengthened his emotional ties to those he loved.

Focusing on the "Why"

Kofi's deep sense of purpose is another key element in his ability to balance without guilt. His ultimate "why" was clear: everything he did in Dubai was for his family's future. This clarity helped him overcome moments of doubt, exhaustion, and guilt, especially when he had to prioritize meetings or business plans over family time.

In Kofi's case, he didn't shy away from explaining his business plans to his children, making them a part of the journey. When his daughter Adjoa asked when he would be home to take her to the park, his response wasn't vague or dismissive. Instead, he used the opportunity to explain how his work would bring them together in the future. This transparency not only reassured his family but also helped Kofi stay grounded in his mission.

By anchoring yourself in your reason for building a business, you can shift your focus from guilt to purpose. Every time Kofi felt torn between his duties as a father and an entrepreneur, he centered himself by remembering that his actions were all for his family's long-term benefit.

Structuring Time and Setting Boundaries

Another way Kofi applied the *Balance Without Guilt* rule was through conscious time management. He structured his day so that he could dedicate certain times for family connection and other times solely to his business. Even from afar, he scheduled regular calls with Ama and the kids, ensuring that his relationship with them wasn't neglected.

In his business dealings, Kofi set clear boundaries. While he worked tirelessly to build his import-export business, he ensured that his work did not entirely overshadow his family. He resisted the urge to overwork by making specific time for his family, even if it was virtual.

Take a Moment to Reflect

Reflection Questions:

- Are you setting clear boundaries between work and family time? Are you scheduling regular check-ins with loved ones, no matter where they are?

- Do you have a clear plan for the future that involves your family? How does that plan motivate you to keep striving for balance?

- How am I maintaining a strong emotional connection with my family, even while building my business abroad?

- Am I clear about my "why," and does my family understand the deeper purpose behind my work?

- Have I structured my time in a way that respects both my business and my family life?

- What long-term plans are motivating me, and how can they help me push through moments of doubt or guilt?

By reflecting on these questions, you can apply the *Balance Without Guilt* rule in your own entrepreneurial journey. Like Kofi, it's possible to pursue your dreams while maintaining a meaningful connection with your family—without letting guilt hold you back. You can find harmony, knowing that both your business and your family are essential parts of your success story.

Action Steps:

- **Set Clear Boundaries**: Use tools like Google Calendar to block specific times for work, family, and self-care. Communicate these boundaries to colleagues and clients to ensure they are respected.

- **Involve Your Family**: Find ways to include your children in your work activities. This could be through age-appropriate tasks or simply sharing what you're working on, helping them understand and appreciate your efforts.

- **Create a Routine**: Establish a daily routine that clearly delineates time for work and time for family. Ensure that both receive your full attention during their designated times.

- **Reflect on Your 'Why'**: Regularly remind yourself of the reasons behind your entrepreneurial journey. Share these motivations with your family to reinforce the shared goals you are working towards.

By implementing these steps, you can create a harmonious balance between your professional pursuits and personal life, ensuring that both thrive together.

A Difficult but Worthy Goal

As you navigate the complexities of balancing family life with entrepreneurial ambitions, remember that this journey is as much about creating meaningful connections as it is about achieving professional success. By setting clear boundaries and involving your loved ones in your endeavors, you can transform the challenges of building a business abroad into opportunities for growth and togetherness. Your commitment to both your family and your business will not only inspire those around you but also pave the way for a fulfilling and balanced life.

PART II

Expanding Your Global Reach

CHAPTER 5:

Spot Opportunities Across Borders

"The world is full of opportunities. Don't wait for them to come to you—go out and find them."

–Richard Branson

The bustling streets of Xintiandi in Shanghai pulsed with energy as I weaved my way through the crowd, my mind alive with possibilities. I had embraced the expat lifestyle, but that morning I realized it's more than adapting to a new culture. It was an opportunity to build something bigger, to think globally. I had overlooked the interconnections of the world. And after just returning from a trip to visit my husband's family in Serbia, I was supercharged with ideas.

That morning, I was heading to a networking event for expats in Shanghai. As I entered the venue, the buzz of conversations in various languages filled the air. I made my way to the refreshment table, pouring myself a cup of green tea, when I overheard a conversation in Serbian.

Intrigued, I turned to see two men engaged in an animated discussion about import regulations. Without hesitation, I approached them, greeting them in Serbian—a language I had picked up from Nemanja over the years.

"Dobro Jutro!" I said with a smile. (Good morning!)

The men's faces lit up, pleasantly surprised to hear their native language from an unexpected source. They introduced themselves as Marko and Stefan, Serbian entrepreneurs who had recently moved to Shanghai to explore business opportunities.

As we chatted, I learned that Marko and Stefan were struggling to navigate the complex landscape of Chinese business regulations. Their innovative food import business had great potential in the Chinese market, but they were hitting roadblocks at every turn.

My mind raced. My years of experience in China, combined with my American business acumen and my connection to Serbia through Nemanja, suddenly seemed like the perfect storm of expertise to help these men succeed.

"You know," I said, my eyes sparkling with excitement, "I think I might help you. I've been working in international trade for several years, and I've learned a thing or two about navigating the Chinese market. Plus, my husband's Serbian background gives me a unique understanding of where you're coming from."

Marko and Stefan exchanged glances, their interest piqued. "That would be incredible," Marko said. "But why would you want to help us?"

I paused for a moment, considering the question. It was in that instant that the idea crystallized in my mind. "Because," I said slowly, "I think this could be the start of something much bigger than just helping you two. I think we might be onto a genuine opportunity here."

Over the next few weeks, I threw myself into helping Marko and Stefan. I introduced them to my network of Chinese businesspeople, helped them understand the nuances of local business culture, and used my trade compliance background to refine their market entry strategy.

As I worked with the Serbian duo, my vision expanded. I saw connections not just between America, Serbia, and China, but with other countries as well. Seeking expertise and resources, I contacted my former colleagues in the United States. I connected with Nemanja's friends back in Serbia, gaining insights into European markets and regulations.

The more I branched out, the more I realized that my actual strength lay in my ability to see the big picture—to think globally rather than just bilaterally. I wasn't just bridging two cultures; I was creating a web of international connections that spanned continents.

Inspired by this revelation, I continued to grow my network of Serbian contacts.

Years later, when we moved to Dubai, my network continued to grow exponentially. I worked with people from every corner of the globe, each bringing their own unique perspectives and opportunities. I helped register businesses in mid-shore and offshore countries, navigating the complex world of tech, international business, and compliance regulations.

One day, as I sat in my home office overlooking the Dubai skyline, I reflected on the journey that had brought me there. My chance meeting in Shanghai highlighted the significance of a global perspective for me. My mind wandered to the people I'd connected, the companies I'd helped create, and the bridges I'd built between different cultures and nations.

I realized that my success wasn't just about my skills or my experience. It was about my willingness to look beyond the obvious connections, to see the world not as a collection of isolated countries, but as an interconnected web of opportunities.

My phone buzzed, interrupting my reverie. It was an email from a potential new client—a Ghanian tech startup looking to expand into the Middle East. As

I read the message, I felt that familiar excitement bubbling up inside me. Another opportunity to bridge cultures, to connect dots that others might not see.

As I typed my response, I smiled to myself. This was what it meant to think big, to think globally. It wasn't just about being an expat, or about connecting two countries. It was about seeing the entire world as your playground, recognizing that in today's interconnected globe, opportunities know no borders.

My journey from an American expat in China to a global business connector in Dubai was more than just a career path. It was a testament to the power of embracing a truly global mindset. In a world that often seems divided, I had found success by bringing people together, by helping others see the possibilities that emerge when you think beyond borders.

As I clicked send on my reply to the Ghanian startup, I felt a sense of excitement about what the future held. I knew that every new connection, every new country I engaged with, would only expand my vision further. In the global business landscape, I had found not just a career, but a calling.

And it all started with a simple realization: in today's world, thinking big means thinking globally.

Rule: Think Big, Think Global

After sharing my personal journey from an American expat in China to a global business connector in Dubai, it's clear that the key to my success lies in two fundamental principles: Think Big and Think Global. Let's explore each of these concepts in depth.

Think Big

Thinking big means not limiting yourself to what you've done previously. It's about seeing the connections between all of your talents and understanding how they can benefit you in ways you might not have initially imagined.

As an expat entrepreneur, you have a unique advantage. Your experiences across different cultures and countries have given you a perspective that few others possess. Thinking big means leveraging this perspective to its fullest potential.

Start by taking stock of all your skills and experiences. Don't just focus on your professional background–consider everything you've learned from living in different countries, navigating diverse cultures, and overcoming the challenges of expat life. Each of these experiences has taught you valuable lessons and given you skills that can be applied in innovative ways.

Challenge yourself to think beyond your current role or business. How can you combine your various skills and experiences to create something truly unique? For instance, my background in tech, combined with my experience in China and my connection to Serbia through my husband, allowed me to see opportunities that others might have missed.

Thinking big also means being open to possibilities that might seem unconventional at first. Don't be afraid to connect seemingly unrelated ideas or industries. Some of the most innovative businesses come from unexpected combinations of skills and knowledge.

Remember, as an expat, you have a multifaceted identity. You're not just a professional in your field–you're also a cultural bridge, a language learner, an adapter, and a problem solver. Thinking big means embracing all these aspects of your identity and using them to your advantage.

Think Global

While thinking big expands the scope of what you can do, thinking global expands where you can do it. As an expat, you already have a head start in global thinking. You are living proof that business and life don't have to be confined to one country. But true global thinking goes beyond just your home and host countries.

Start by considering all the countries where you have some kind of connection, no matter how tenuous. Perhaps you studied abroad in college, have distant relatives in another country, or worked on a project with international partners. Each of these connections is a potential gateway to new opportunities.

But don't stop there. In today's interconnected world, you can create connections with almost any country. The key is to stay curious and open-minded. Research emerging markets, follow international business news, and always be on the lookout for global trends that you could tap into.

Thinking globally also means understanding that different markets have different needs. What works in one country might need to be adapted for another. Your experience as an expat gives you a head start in understanding these nuances, but it's important to continue learning and expanding your cultural fluency.

Leverage your international networks. As an expat, you're likely part of a diverse community. Each person in your network is a potential connection to new markets and opportunities. Don't underestimate the power of these connections–they can provide invaluable insights, introductions, and partnerships.

Finally, thinking globally means being prepared to operate across borders. This might involve understanding international business regulations, being comfortable with different business cultures, or even learning new languages. It's about developing the skills and mindset to see the entire world as your potential market.

By combining these two principles–thinking big and thinking global–you can unlock opportunities you might never have considered before. It's not just about expanding your business; it's about expanding your vision of what's possible.

In the next section, we'll explore some practical strategies for implementing this "Think Big, Think Global" mindset on your own entrepreneurial journey.

CASE STUDY: KYLE'S MULTICULTURAL ADVANTAGE

Kyle, a 20-year-old college student, had always stood out from the crowd. Born to a Chinese mother and a Black American father, he had spent his childhood moving between various countries due to his parents' expat assignments. This nomadic upbringing had gifted him with fluency in both English and Chinese, as well as an innate ability to adapt to new environments.

Despite his global background, Kyle had made the unexpected choice to attend a Historically Black College and University (HBCU) in the United States. There, he excelled in Chinese Studies, leveraging his background while immersing himself in a unique cultural experience.

As his sophomore year drew to a close, Kyle found himself at a crossroads. Two summer opportunities lay before him: a prestigious language program in China that aligned perfectly with his major, and an internship with a global consulting firm in Madrid, Spain. The choice seemed obvious too many of Kyle's peers and professors. The China program would allow him to deepen his expertise in a familiar field, leveraging his language skills and cultural knowledge.

But Kyle surprised everyone by choosing the internship in Spain. "I already know China," he explained to his bewildered advisors. "I want to see what else is out there. I want to challenge myself to adapt to a completely new environment and see how I can apply my skills in an unexpected context."

In the weeks leading up to his departure, Kyle threw himself into preparation. He began learning basic Spanish, researched Spain's position in the global economy, and read up on the basics of consulting. He set ambitious goals for himself, not just for the internship, but for how this experience could shape his future career trajectory.

Arriving in Madrid was a shock to the system. The rapid-fire Spanish, the late-night dinners, the afternoon siestas—everything was new and challenging. At the consulting firm, Kyle initially felt out of his depth. His colleagues were from top business schools, fluent in multiple European languages, and well-versed in consulting frameworks that Kyle had never encountered.

But as the weeks went by, Kyle found his footing. He volunteered for a challenging project aimed at helping a Spanish company expand into Asian markets. Drawing on his knowledge of Chinese business practices, Kyle offered insights that his colleagues hadn't considered. His unique perspective, combining Eastern and Western viewpoints, led to innovative solutions that impressed both the team and the client.

Kyle's background from the HBCU also proved unexpectedly valuable. When a client wanted to improve their diversity and inclusion practices globally, Kyle drew on his experiences to offer nuanced suggestions that went beyond surface-level solutions.

As his Spanish improved, Kyle acted as a bridge between cultures. He helped his European colleagues understand the nuances of communicating with Chinese businesses, while also explaining American business practices to Spanish clients looking to expand across the Atlantic.

By the end of the summer, Kyle had not only gained valuable consulting experience but had also expanded his global perspective far beyond his expectations. He had become conversational in Spanish, adding a third language to his global toolkit. He had built a network that spanned continents, with colleagues and clients from Europe, Asia, and the Americas.

The consulting firm, impressed by Kyle's unique contributions and adaptability, offered him a part-time remote position during his studies and a fast-track to a global graduate program upon graduation. More importantly, this experience had transformed Kyle's view of his own potential and the opportunities available in the global marketplace.

Key Points: How Kyle Applied "Think Big, Think Global"

Thinking Big:

- By choosing the less obvious path, Kyle demonstrated his willingness to push beyond his comfort zone and existing expertise.

- He reframed his perceived weaknesses (lack of Spanish skills, no consulting experience) as opportunities for rapid growth.

- Kyle leveraged his unique background in unexpected ways, bringing insights from his Chinese Studies and HBCU experience to the world of global consulting.

Thinking Global:

- Kyle's choice to go to Spain rather than China showed his understanding that global thinking means being open to opportunities anywhere in the world, not just in familiar contexts.

- He actively sought to understand Spain's business culture, recognizing that each country has its unique approach to global commerce.

- Kyle positioned himself as a bridge between European, American, and Asian business cultures, adding value to international projects.

- By learning Spanish and immersing himself in a new culture, Kyle expanded his global skill set and perspective.

Combining Big and Global Thinking:

Kyle's approach to challenges exemplified both big and global thinking. When faced with difficult projects, he saw them as opportunities to expand his skills and global understanding. He combined elements of Eastern philosophy, Western business practices, and diverse cultural insights to develop creative solutions for clients. By actively connecting with colleagues and clients from diverse backgrounds, Kyle built a truly global professional network that will serve him well in future endeavors.

Kyle's summer experience shows that thinking big and thinking globally often go hand in hand. By pushing himself to explore beyond his areas of expertise and comfort, Kyle not only grew personally and professionally but also positioned himself as a valuable asset in the global marketplace.

Take a Moment to Reflect

Reflection Points:

1. **Cultural Bridge**: Reflect on a time when you successfully bridged two different cultures, either in a personal or professional context. What specific skills or attitudes enabled you to do this effectively? How could you apply these on a larger, global scale?

2. **Unexpected Connections**: Think about your most diverse experiences (e.g., your American background, Serbian connections, and time in China). What unexpected synergies or insights arise when you consider these experiences together? How might these unique combinations create value in a global business context?

3. **Comfort Zone Expansion**: Consider Kyle's decision to intern in Spain rather than China. What would be your equivalent "Spain"—an opportunity that would push you out of your comfort zone but potentially lead to significant growth? What fears or limiting beliefs might hold you back from pursuing such opportunities?

4. **Five-Year Vision**: Imagine yourself five years from now as a successful global entrepreneur. What does your business or career look like? What new skills, connections, or experiences have you gained? How has your

global mindset expanded? Use this vision to identify concrete steps you can take today to move towards this future.

Action Steps:

Here are four actionable steps to help you think big and think globally. These steps expand your global perspective, leverage your unique experiences, and identify international opportunities. By completing these tasks, you'll be better equipped to think and act on a global scale.

- **Create Your Global Network Map**: Start by using a world map, either physical or digital, to visually represent your international connections. Mark all countries where you have ties, including family, friends, work, and educational connections. For each connection, make a note about its nature and potential value. This exercise will help you visualize your existing global reach and identify areas where your network could be expanded.

- **Perform a Global Skills Audit**: List all your skills, experiences, and knowledge areas, including those that might seem unrelated to your current work. For each item on your list, brainstorm potential global applications. This process will help you identify unique skill combinations that could provide a competitive edge in the international market. Additionally, it will highlight which skills you may need to develop further for global success.

- **Undertake a Cultural Immersion Challenge**: Select an unfamiliar country that has potential business opportunities and commit to a one-month immersion. Learn at least twenty basic phrases in the local language, follow local news sources daily, or watch a few films or TV shows from that culture. Make an effort to connect with at least three locals or expats from that country. Throughout this process, document your learnings and insights to reflect on your growing global perspective.

- **Conceptualize a Global Business Idea**: Using the insights gained from the previous steps, brainstorm five potential global business ideas. Select the most promising concept and outline how it solves a problem that spans multiple countries or cultures. Describe how your unique background and experiences give you an advantage in implementing this idea. Finally, create a one-page pitch for your global business concept, synthesizing all you've learned through this process.

By completing these action steps, you'll be taking concrete strides toward developing a global mindset and identifying unique opportunities in the international business landscape.

Conclusion: Think Big, Think Global

In this chapter, we've explored the transformative power of adopting a "Think Big, Think Global" mindset for expat entrepreneurs.

We focused on two key principles:

- **Think Big**: This concept encourages expat entrepreneurs to see the connections between all their talents and experiences, challenging them to think beyond their current role or business. It's about embracing your multifaceted identity as an expat and using it to your advantage.

- **Think Global**: This principle expands the scope of where you can apply your skills and ideas. It involves considering all your international connections, staying curious about global trends, and being prepared to operate across borders.

We then explored practical strategies for implementing this mindset, emphasizing the importance of conducting a personal global audit, expanding global knowledge, leveraging unique backgrounds, and building a global network.

The case study of Kyle, a young college student with a diverse background, brought these principles to life. By choosing an unexpected internship in Spain over a more obvious opportunity in China, Kyle demonstrated how thinking big and thinking globally can lead to innovative solutions, rapid personal growth, and exciting career prospects.

As we conclude this chapter, it's clear that the "Think Big, Think Global" mindset is more than just a strategy for business success, it's a way of approaching life that can open up a world of opportunities. In today's interconnected world, the ability to think beyond borders, to see connections where others see divisions, and to leverage diverse experiences and perspectives is invaluable.

For expat entrepreneurs, this mindset is powerful. Your international experiences, your ability to adapt to new cultures, and your unique perspective are not just personal attributes, they're your competitive advantage in the global marketplace. By thinking big and thinking globally, you can transform challenges into opportunities, bridge cultural divides, and create innovative solutions to global problems.

Remember, adopting this mindset is a journey, not a destination. It requires continuous learning, openness to new experiences, and the courage to step outside your comfort zone. But as we've seen through the stories and examples in this chapter, the rewards can be extraordinary.

As you move forward in your expat entrepreneurial journey, challenge yourself to think bigger and more globally. How can you leverage your unique background to create value on a global scale? What unexpected connections can you make between your skills, experiences, and global opportunities? By asking these questions and embracing the "Think Big, Think Global" mindset, you're not just preparing for success in the global marketplace—you're positioning yourself to make a meaningful impact on the world.

In a world that is increasingly interconnected yet often divided, expat entrepreneurs who can think big and think globally are uniquely positioned to build bridges, drive innovation, and create positive change. As you apply the principles and strategies we've discussed, remember that your global perspective is not just an asset, it's a superpower. Use it wisely, think big, think globally, and watch as a world of opportunities unfolds before you.

CHAPTER 6

Your Global Network Blueprint

"Your network is your net worth."

–Porter Gale

The plush purple seating of the W Hotel rooftop lounge on the Palm in Dubai was almost too comfortable as I sat, anxiously waiting for the invitees to show up. My rum and coke barely quelled the butterflies in my stomach. Through the floor-to-ceiling windows, the sun was setting over the Arabian Gulf, painting the sky in hues of orange and pink. The view was breathtaking, but my eyes remained glued to the entrance, waiting for unfamiliar faces.

I glanced at my watch for the hundredth time. It was 6:55 PM, and my "Women in Web3" event was set to begin in five minutes. I had meticulously organized and promoted it, sending invitations into the void of Dubai's tech scene, hoping to meet like-minded women in a city that often felt isolating. With so many male-dominated Web3 events that didn't quite resonate with me, I created the network I wanted—one that focused on women in this space.

As I sat there, doubt crept in. Would anyone show up? Just a few months ago, I had arrived in Dubai with ambition, but no local connections. Now, here I was, wondering if this event would be the key to changing that. At 7:05 PM, a woman walked in, looking around uncertainly. My heart leaped as I jumped up, maybe a bit too eagerly, to introduce myself. Soon after, a small trickle of attendees became a group. By 7:15, we had enough women to begin meaningful conversations, and relief washed over me as I watched connections form.

That night was just one of many "Women in Web3" events I would organize. Each gathering brought its own mix of challenges and successes. Some nights were electric, full of energy and ideas, while others were quieter, where only a handful of women showed up. I remember one particularly rough evening when a sandstorm hit Dubai, and only two women braved the weather. Despite the small turnout, we had an intimate and delightful conversation. Even so, I knew that building a sustainable network was harder than I had expected.

The consistency, though, was key. Month after month, I organized these events, choosing venues, creating Eventbrite listings, and inviting people. Sometimes I felt like I was taking two steps forward, one step back. While I enjoyed seeing connections form, I didn't yet have a strategy for fostering ongoing relationships beyond the meetups.

That's when I stumbled upon *The 2-Hour Cocktail Party* by Nick Gray, a book that would shift my approach to networking. Inspired by its simplicity, I tried a more intimate style of gathering. Instead of the usual hotel lounges, I hosted a small group of women in my apartment one evening. The view of the Dubai Marina skyline set the perfect backdrop as we gathered in my living room. Some attendees were familiar faces from previous Web3 events, while others were new acquaintances.

The atmosphere was different—more relaxed and personal. Conversations flowed more easily, and connections seemed to form naturally. A UX designer and a blockchain developer discovered they were working on complementary projects, and two other women realized they had attended the same university in the U.S., though years apart. Watching these connections unfold in my own home felt like a major step forward.

Encouraged by the success of that evening, I began hosting more intimate gatherings in my home. These cocktail parties allowed for deeper connections, complementing the larger Web3 events I was still organizing. My network in Dubai grew organically, and my phone contacts slowly filled with local numbers, each representing a meaningful connection.

But I wasn't satisfied with just local connections. Recognizing the importance of expanding my reach, I launched a podcast as a new way to connect. Through each episode, I interviewed fascinating people in the tech world, both in Dubai and beyond. The podcast opened doors I hadn't anticipated—conversations with guests turned into collaborations, and listeners from around the globe began reaching out.

Looking back at those early days of sitting anxiously in hotel lounges, waiting for strangers to show up, I'm amazed at how far I've come. The cocktail parties, podcast interviews, and events built my network not just in Dubai, but globally.

What I learned from my journey is that networking isn't about perfection. It's about showing up, consistently creating opportunities for connection, and being open to where those connections might lead. Most importantly, it's about taking initiative, especially in a new place, and knowing that with time, persistence, and creativity, a strong and supportive network can be built from scratch.

Rule: Build Your Global Network from the Ground Up

After a series of fails and successes in network building in Dubai, I want to distill the lessons I've learned into actionable strategies that you can apply in your own expat journey. While every situation is unique, these four key approaches have proven invaluable in my experience and can serve as a solid foundation for building your network in a new country.

Identify a Niche and Become an Organizer

One of the most powerful ways to build a network is to position yourself at the center. Instead of waiting for opportunities to come to you, create them yourself by becoming an event organizer in a specific niche.

In my case, I noticed a gap in the Dubai tech scene: a lack of networking events specifically for women in Web3. By identifying this niche and organizing events around it, I not only filled a need in the community but also established myself as a leader and connector in this space.

When choosing your niche, look for an intersection between your interests, your expertise, and an unmet need in your new community. It could be anything from "Expat Entrepreneurs in FinTech" to "Sustainable Fashion Professionals" or "International Educators in STEM." The key is to be specific enough to attract a dedicated group, but broad enough to ensure a good turnout.

Once you've identified your niche, start small. Your first event doesn't need to be a grand affair. Begin with a casual coffee meetup or a small discussion group. As you gain confidence and your network grows, you can scale up to larger events, workshops, or panel discussions.

Remember, as an organizer, you're not just an attendee, you're a leader. This role comes with responsibilities, but also with significant benefits. You'll can shape the conversation, make introductions, and be the person everyone wants to know. It's a powerful position that can accelerate your network-building efforts dramatically.

Be Consistent and Persistent

Building a network, especially in a new country, is not a onetime effort. It requires consistency and persistence. When I first started organizing "Women in Web3" events in Dubai, there were nights when only a handful of people showed up. It would have been easy to get discouraged and give up. But I knew that building something meaningful takes time, so I persisted.

Consistency is key in network building. Whether you're organizing events, creating content, or simply reaching out to new contacts, make it a regular part of your routine. Set a schedule and stick to it. For instance, commit to hosting an event every month, or posting on your professional social media accounts three times a week.

This consistency serves multiple purposes. First, it helps people remember you and your initiatives. When people see your name or your event series pop up regularly, it becomes part of their mental landscape. Second, it gives you multiple chances to succeed. Not every event will be a hit, not every post will go viral, but by consistently putting yourself out there, you increase your chances of making meaningful connections.

Persistence is equally important. There will be setbacks. Events with low turnout, unanswered emails, networking attempts that fall flat. Don't let these discourage you. Instead, view them as learning opportunities. After each networking effort, take some time to reflect. What worked well? What could be improved? Use these insights to refine your approach.

Remember, every person you meet, every conversation you have, is a step forward in building your network. Celebrate small wins, learn from experiences, and keep moving forward The network you build through consistent, persistent effort will be far stronger and more valuable than any connections you might make through a single, large networking event.

Embrace Digital Platforms

In today's interconnected world, your networking efforts shouldn't be limited to face-to-face interactions. Digital platforms offer powerful tools to expand your reach, showcase your expertise, and stay connected with your growing network.

Social media platforms like LinkedIn, Twitter, and Instagram can be invaluable for professional networking. Each platform has its strengths, so choose the ones that best align with your goals and where your target network is most active. On LinkedIn, for example, you can share professional insights, engage with industry content, and directly connect with colleagues in your field. Twitter can be great for joining real-time conversations about your industry, while Instagram might be perfect for giving a behind-the-scenes look at your professional life or events.

Don't just use these platforms to broadcast; engage authentically. Comment on others' posts, share valuable content, and be part of the conversation. This consistent, genuine engagement can help you build a strong online presence and attract potential connections.

Beyond social media, consider leveraging other digital tools. Event management platforms like Eventbrite or Meetup can help you organize and promote your events while tapping into existing communities. You might also consider starting a newsletter to keep your network informed about your initiatives and insights.

In my experience, one particularly effective digital networking tool was podcasting. By starting a podcast, I could connect with interesting people in the tech and business world, both in Dubai and globally. Each episode became an opportunity not just to create content, but to build a relationship with my guest and provide value to my listeners.

Remember, your digital presence is often the first impression you'll make on potential connections. Ensure that it accurately reflects your professional brand and the value you bring to your network.

Be Vulnerable with Content Creation

While it might seem counterintuitive, being vulnerable in your content creation can be a powerful way to build authentic connections. By sharing not just your successes but also your challenges and learning experiences, you make yourself more relatable and approachable.

Content creation–whether it's through a blog, podcast, videos, or social media posts–allows you to showcase your expertise while also revealing your personality. It's an opportunity to demonstrate your knowledge and insights, but also to show the human behind the professional facade.

In my journey, starting a podcast was a significant step in this direction. It required me to put myself out there, to have public conversations, and to share my thoughts and opinions with a potentially global audience. This felt vulnerable, especially at first, but it also opened doors to connections and opportunities I never could have anticipated.

When creating content, don't be afraid to share your experiences, including the difficulties and setbacks. Talk about the challenges of building a business in a new country, the cultural misunderstandings you've navigated, or the lessons you've learned from your mistakes. This kind of honest, vulnerable content resonates with people and can help you build a loyal, engaged network.

However, being vulnerable doesn't mean oversharing or being unprofessional. It's about finding the right balance, sharing enough of your personal journey to be authentic and relatable, while still maintaining your professional image.

Also, remember that content creation is not just about what you share, but how you engage with your audience. Respond to comments, ask for feedback, and be open to discussions. This two-way interaction is what transforms content consumers into genuine connections.

By implementing these four strategies–becoming a niche organizer, maintaining consistency and persistence, embracing digital platforms, and being vulnerable in your content creation—you'll be well on your way to building a strong, authentic network in your new country. Remember, network building is a journey, not a destination. Enjoy the process, learn from every interaction, and watch as your global network grows and flourishes.

CASE STUDY: ANGELA'S NETWORK BUILDING JOURNEY IN HONG KONG

Angela Brown stood at the window of her small Hong Kong apartment, gazing out at the glittering skyline. Six months ago, this 32-year-old FinTech professional from New York had jumped at the chance to join a promising blockchain startup in Asia's financial hub. With her background in cryptocurrency and her passion for innovation, it had seemed like the perfect move. Yet tonight, like many nights before, she felt a gnawing sense of isolation.

Hong Kong was everything she had expected—bustling, vibrant, filled with opportunity. The FinTech scene was indeed happening, with events and meetups occurring almost every night. But something was missing. The networking events she'd attended felt impersonal, dominated by large financial institutions rather than the startup culture she craved. Despite being surrounded by millions of people, Angela felt alone.

As she scrolled through her phone, declining yet another invitation to a corporate networking event, Angela had an epiphany. If she couldn't find the community she was looking for, why not create it herself? She thought about what she really wanted—a space for women like her, passionate about cryptocurrency and blockchain, to connect and support each other.

With a mix of excitement and trepidation, Angela created an event on Meetup.com: "CryptoWomen HK: Coffee and Blockchain Chat." She chose a cozy cafe in Central, hoping that at least a few women would show up. To her surprise and delight, fifteen women attended that first meetup.

The energy in the room was palpable as they shared their experiences, challenges, and aspirations in the crypto world.

Encouraged by the positive response, Angela decided to make it a regular thing. She committed to hosting monthly events, alternating between casual coffee meetups and more structured panel discussions or workshops. It wasn't always easy. There were nights when only a handful of people showed up, and Angela questioned whether it was worth continuing. But she persisted, reminding herself that building a community takes time.

Her persistence paid off. By the sixth month, her events were regularly attracting 30-40 attendees. She started receiving messages from women thanking her for creating this space, sharing how the connections made through CryptoWomen HK had led to job opportunities, collaborations, and friendships.

As the community grew, Angela realized she needed to expand beyond physical meetups. She created a LinkedIn group for CryptoWomen HK, providing a space for members to connect between events, share job opportunities, and discuss industry news. She also started an X account (previously Twitter) where she shared event updates, industry insights, and highlighted the achievements of women in Hong Kong's crypto scene.

Managing the growing community pushed Angela out of her comfort zone. She found herself public speaking more often, improving her skills with each event. She learned to facilitate discussions, making sure every voice was heard. The role of organizer challenged her, but also filled her with a sense of purpose she hadn't felt since moving to Hong Kong.

Inspired by the conversations at her events, Angela decided to start a blog called "Crypto Chronicles: A Woman's Journey in Blockchain." Here, she shared not just technical insights about cryptocurrency, but also her personal experiences as a woman in the industry and an expat in Hong Kong. She wrote about the challenges of adapting to a new work culture, the times she felt out of her depth in meetings, and her ongoing efforts to understand the local FinTech landscape.

Writing the blog made Angela feel vulnerable. She was putting herself out there, sharing her struggles alongside her successes. But to her surprise, this vulnerability resonated deeply with her readers. Comments poured in from women facing similar challenges, thanking her for giving voice to their experiences.

As her blog gained traction, Angela was invited to speak at other events and contribute to industry publications. She was initially nervous about this increased visibility, but found that sharing her authentic experiences helped her connect more deeply with her growing network.

One year after that first coffee meetup, Angela stood at the podium of a major FinTech conference in Hong Kong, preparing to give a keynote speech on women in blockchain. As she looked out at the audience, she saw many familiar faces—women she'd met through CryptoWomen HK, readers of her blog, colleagues from across the industry.

In that moment, Angela realized how far she'd come. From feeling isolated and out of place, she had become a recognized figure in Hong Kong's women in FinTech community. Her network had grown exponentially, spanning not just cryptocurrency, but the broader industry. CryptoWomen HK events now regularly attracted 50-60 attendees, with a waiting list. Her blog had grown into a popular resource, with a monthly readership of over 10,000.

The connections she'd made led to exciting opportunities. She had partnered with two women she met through CryptoWomen HK to launch a blockchain education initiative for high school girls. She'd been headhunted for a senior role at a leading crypto exchange and invited to join the board of a non-profit focused on promoting diversity in FinTech.

Most importantly, Angela no longer felt out of place in Hong Kong. She had created a community where she and others like her could thrive. The city that once felt overwhelming now felt full of opportunities and connections. As she began her speech, Angela smiled, feeling truly at home for the first time since she'd arrived in Hong Kong.

Key Points in Angela's Network Building Journey

Angela Brown's experience in Hong Kong demonstrates the practical application of the four key strategies for building a network in a foreign country. Let's examine how she implemented each strategy:

Identify a Niche and Become an Organizer

Angela applied this strategy by:

- Recognizing a gap in Hong Kong's FinTech scene: a lack of networking opportunities specifically for women in cryptocurrency and blockchain.

- Creating "CryptoWomen HK," a networking group tailored to this niche.

- Starting with a small, manageable event (a coffee meetup) and gradually expanding to larger, more structured gatherings.

- Positioning herself as a leader and facilitator in this community, rather than just an attendee.

Result: Angela transformed from an isolated newcomer to a central figure in Hong Kong's women in FinTech community.

Be Consistent and Persistent

Angela demonstrated consistency and persistence by:

- Committing to hosting monthly CryptoWomen HK events, regardless of initial turnout.

- Continuing her efforts even when attendance was low, recognizing that building a community takes time.

- Regularly following up with new connections and sharing relevant content between events.

- Gradually increasing the frequency and scale of events as the community grew.

Result: After six months, her events were regularly attracting 30-40 attendees, growing to 50-60 by the end of her first year.

Embrace Digital Platforms

Angela leveraged digital platforms by:

- Creating a LinkedIn group for CryptoWomen HK to facilitate ongoing connections and discussions.

- Starting a social media account to share updates, insights, and highlight community achievements.

- Using Eventbrite or similar platforms to manage event registrations and increase visibility.

- Experimenting with virtual events to expand reach and feature international speakers.

Result: Angela expanded her network beyond physical event attendees, attracting followers and connections from across Asia and globally.

Be Vulnerable with Content Creation

Angela embraced vulnerability in her content creation by:

- Starting a blog, "Crypto Chronicles: A Woman's Journey in Blockchain," where she shared both professional insights and personal experiences.

- Writing openly about her challenges as an expat and a woman in the FinTech industry.

- Sharing her struggles and moments of self-doubt alongside her successes.

- Using her experiences as material for speeches and contributions to industry publications.

Result: Angela's vulnerability resonated deeply with her audience, leading to stronger connections, speaking opportunities, and a monthly blog readership of over 10,000.

By consistently applying these four strategies, Angela transformed her experience in Hong Kong. She went from feeling isolated and out of place to becoming a recognized leader in her field, with a thriving professional network and numerous opportunities for collaboration and career advancement. Her journey illustrates how these strategies can effectively build a strong, supportive network in a new country, even when starting from scratch in an unfamiliar environment.

Take a Moment to Reflect

Reflection Questions:

1. What unique perspective or expertise can you bring to your professional community in your new location? How does your background as an expatriate contribute to this?

2. What fears or hesitations do you have about putting yourself out there as an event organizer or content creator? How can you address these concerns?

3. Think about a time when you felt out of place or isolated in your new location. What kind of community or support would have made a difference at that moment?

4. How has your definition of "networking" changed after reading about Angela's journey? What new approaches to building professional relationships are you considering?

Action Steps

- **Identify Your Niche**: Choose a specific area within your field or interests where you can create value. Research existing groups and events in your new location to find gaps you could fill.

- **Plan Your First Event**: Organize a small, manageable event in your identified niche. It could be as simple as a coffee meetup or an online discussion group. Set a date, find a venue (physical or virtual), and create an event listing.

- **Establish Your Online Presence**: Choose one or two digital platforms that are popular in your new location. Create a professional profile or page related to your niche. Start sharing relevant content and insights regularly.

- **Create Vulnerable Content**: Start a blog, vlog, or podcast where you can share your professional insights along with your personal experiences as an expatriate. Commit to creating and publishing content on a consistent schedule.

Conclusion: Building Your Network Abroad

As we've explored in this chapter, building a professional network in a foreign country can be one of the most challenging yet rewarding aspects of an expatriate's journey. Through our examination of four key strategies and Angela Brown's inspiring story, we've uncovered valuable insights into how to approach this crucial task.

We began by discussing the importance of identifying a niche and becoming an organizer. This strategy allows you to position yourself at the center of a community, filling gaps in the local professional landscape and establishing yourself as a leader. Angela's creation of CryptoWomen HK exemplifies how this approach can transform an isolated individual into a central figure in their field.

Next, we emphasized the critical role of consistency and persistence. Building a network is not an overnight process; it requires ongoing effort and resilience in the face of initial setbacks. Angela's commitment to regular events, even when attendance was low, ultimately led to a thriving community.

We then explored the power of digital platforms in expanding and maintaining your network. In today's interconnected world, your networking efforts should extend beyond face-to-face interactions. By leveraging social media, professional networking sites, and content creation platforms, you can reach a wider audience and stay connected with your growing network.

Finally, we discussed the impact of vulnerability in content creation. Sharing not just your professional insights but also your personal experiences can foster deeper, more meaningful connections. Angela's blog, where she opened up about her challenges as an expat and a woman in FinTech, resonated deeply with her audience and opened doors to new opportunities.

Angela's journey from an isolated newcomer to a recognized leader in Hong Kong's FinTech scene illustrates the transformative power of these strategies when applied consistently and authentically. Her story reminds us that while the path may not always be easy, the rewards of building a strong professional network in a new country are immeasurable.

As you embark on or continue your own networking journey abroad, remember that everyone starts somewhere. Each connection you make, each event you organize, and each piece of content you create is a step towards building the community you seek. Embrace the process, learn from both successes and setbacks, and remain open to the unexpected opportunities that may arise.

Building a network in a foreign country is not just about professional advancement; it's about creating a sense of belonging, finding your tribe in a new place, and potentially making a lasting impact on your adopted community. As you apply the strategies and insights from this chapter, you're not just building a network, you're creating a home for yourself and others in your new world.

Remember, the journey of network building is ongoing. As your network grows and evolves, so too will your role within it. Stay curious, remain authentic, and keep pushing beyond your comfort zone. The connections you forge and the community you build have the power to not only transform your professional life but also to enrich your entire expat experience.

CHAPTER 7

Make It Happen

"An idea not coupled with action will never get any bigger than the brain cell it occupied."

–Arnold Glasow

I t's 5:30 AM, and I wake up before my alarm. I'm a naturally early riser, and I've learned to treasure the quiet hours of the morning when I'm most productive. It's a habit I picked up during my corporate days—before the emails flood in, before the kids are awake, before the demands of the day pile up. This is *my* time. Time to focus, strategize, and set the tone for the day ahead.

The first thing I do after I get out of bed is grab a glass of warm water or tea and hydrate. I then start to fill my mind with optimistic thoughts about my life, my family, and the work that I do. I set my mind to gratitude. From there, it's a mad dash to get my kids ready for school, prepare breakfast and lunches and get them out of the door. It's important for me to feel an upbeat rhythm in my personal life in order for me to be productive in my business so I aim to keep positivity at home. My complete business is mapped out there, from long-term goals to daily tasks. While I'm helping my kids get ready for the day, I'm mentally rehearsing some targets I'd like to accomplish for the day with my own work.

What's on deck for today? Finalize a contract for ByteBao's latest project, outline my next speaking engagement, and create content for my personal brand. *Got it.* These tasks aren't just floating around in my head—they're carefully broken down on my Trello board, each step clear, with deadlines that keep me accountable.

8:00 AM: The Power of Routine

By 8:00 AM, after the school drop-off, I've got my coffee in hand, and I'm at my desk. I'm a big believer in routine—it creates structure in what could otherwise feel like chaos. I open my calendar, the most sacred tool in my toolkit. Every block of time has a purpose. Today, I've set aside two hours for uninterrupted deep work, focusing on finalizing the contract.

My calendar is more than just a list of appointments. It's where I manage my life. I've blocked out time not only for work but also for picking up my kids, cooking dinner, and even relaxing in the evening. If it's not on the calendar, it doesn't happen. It's how I make sure I'm giving enough attention to both ByteBao and my personal brand, as well as my family.

I'm focused on this contract because it's a critical part of ByteBao's growth. ByteBao isn't just a business—it's a reflection of me, my values, and my vision. When I first started the company, I knew I wanted it to be more than just consulting. I wanted it to be an ecosystem that blended my professional expertise in law and emerging technologies with my passion for empowerment and education. But turning that vision into a reality required a lot of discipline. And that discipline starts here—at my desk, with my calendar, Trello board, and coffee.

8:30 AM: Managing Myself, Just Like a Team

By 8:30 AM, I'm ready for the next item on my Trello board. But first, it's time for a quick break to reset. I've learned that managing myself is a lot like managing a team—if you push too hard without breaks, you burn out. A few years ago, when I first left the corporate world, I thought I could just apply the same leadership strategies I used on my teams to myself. I was wrong. It's so much harder to hold *yourself* accountable. There's no one to step in and remind you to get back on track when you get distracted.

I've gotten better at it by using tools like Trello, which I treat as my personal project manager. For example, this morning, I've mapped out not just today's tasks but also my weekly and monthly goals. This lets me see the bigger picture while focusing on what needs to get done right now. It's how I self-manage—by staying clear about where I'm going and what steps I need to take to get there.

After a quick reset, I dive into outlining my next speaking engagement. It's for an international tech conference, where I'll be blending insights from ByteBao with my personal story. This is where my personal brand really comes into play. When I speak, I'm not just representing ByteBao—I'm representing *me*, and that's intentional. My personal brand is intertwined with my business. ByteBao reflects my expertise and my story as an expat entrepreneur navigating global markets. I want the audience to see that ByteBao's mission—empowerment through legal and technological education—reflects who I am as a person.

12:00 PM: Time Management—The Backbone of My Success

Lunch is another scheduled event on my calendar. It may sound extreme, but I've found that if I don't schedule personal activities, they don't happen. If my day is too chaotic, I risk burning out. So, just as I block out time for business meetings, I block out time to eat, pick up my kids, and even go for a walk.

In the afternoon, I have meetings, but everything is scheduled with intention. If I'm working on something critical for ByteBao, I ensure I don't schedule other activities during that time. My calendar reflects my strategy—both personal and professional. Every block of time has a purpose.

By 2:00 PM, I'm back at my desk for a few hours of focused content creation. This is where I'm growing my personal brand. Today, I'm filming short videos about entrepreneurship, technology, and balancing life as an expat businesswoman. I use these videos to engage with my community and share insights about my journey—both the successes and the struggles. ByteBao's success is directly tied to my personal brand because people aren't just buying services—they're buying into the values I represent.

5:00 PM: Measuring Progress and Staying Accountable

By the time evening rolls around, I review my progress. Measuring growth is one of the hardest parts of entrepreneurship—especially for visionaries like me. It's easy to get caught up in new ideas and forget to look back and see how far you've come. That's why I have KPIs (Key Performance Indicators) built into my Trello board and calendar.

Today, I take a look at the metrics for ByteBao—how many contracts have been closed, how many leads we've generated, and how much content I've produced for my personal brand. These numbers aren't just for vanity. They help me see where I'm succeeding and where I need to improve.

I'm always working to be better at holding myself accountable, which is why I revisit my original plan regularly. Have I met my deadlines? Am I on track with my long-term goals? What needs adjusting? This evening, I set aside time to reflect on these questions, going back to my Trello board and calendar to make sure that every move I've made today is aligned with where I want to go.

8:00 PM: The Day Winds Down

By 8:00 PM, I've wrapped up dinner and am spending time with my family. The day may wind down, but the structure I've built stays intact. Tomorrow, I'll wake up again, look at my Trello board, and follow the plan that's been set out—not just for ByteBao, but for me as a person.

Building a business abroad isn't easy. There are days when I feel overwhelmed by the sheer scale of what I want to accomplish. But by creating systems that keep me disciplined, managing my time with precision, and holding myself accountable, I've learned to turn my vision into action, one day at a time.

For the chapter you're working on about turning ambition into action, we can structure the lesson or framework by focusing on the four key pieces you want to communicate: discipline, self-management, time management, and measurable progress. Here's a draft of the lesson based on those elements, tying them to practical strategies for business-building:

Turning Ambition Into Action: Practical Strategies for Success

Building a business abroad requires more than just vision—it demands the relentless discipline to execute that vision. Ambition is the fuel, but action is the engine that moves you forward. The journey to entrepreneurship isn't easy, but by mastering four core strategies, you can turn ambition into sustainable success.

Discipline: Your Foundation for Success

Discipline is the cornerstone of any entrepreneurial endeavor. Without it, even the best ideas remain just that—ideas. It's important to approach discipline as you would any other skill. Start with small commitments and gradually build your capacity to focus and execute consistently.

For expats building a business abroad, discipline is even more critical because you're often working without a built-in support network. The distractions of adapting to a new culture or navigating a foreign bureaucracy can pull you away from your goals. You need to set strict boundaries around your time, energy, and focus.

PRO TIP: Break down your goals into manageable tasks, and commit to finishing one each day, no matter what. Use tools like time-blocking or the Pomodoro technique to ensure you're staying on track.

Rule: Time is Money

In a business, you'd manage a team to ensure everyone is productive and aligned with the company's vision. When you're building your own business, especially as an expat, you are that team. Self-management is about taking full responsibility for your actions, outcomes, and learning.

It's important to hold yourself accountable. Set regular "check-ins" where you reflect on what you've accomplished and adjust where necessary. You must lead yourself with the same rigor and dedication that you'd expect from others.

PRO TIP: Use a project management tool (like Trello, Asana, or Notion) to keep track of your daily, weekly, and monthly goals. Regularly review your progress and be honest with yourself about areas where you need to improve.

Time Management: Maximize Your Most Valuable Resource

Time is the most precious asset you have when building a business. Unlike money, you can't get it back once it's gone. Efficient time management allows you to make steady progress, even when faced with the challenges of living in a foreign country.

Many new entrepreneurs fall into the trap of working long hours without being productive. Instead of simply clocking hours, focus on results. Prioritize tasks that move your business forward and cut out unnecessary distractions. Adaptation is also key—there may be cultural or logistical challenges in your new environment that you'll need to account for.

PRO TIP: Identify your peak productivity hours. Some people work best in the morning, others at night. Structure your most important tasks around these times for maximum efficiency.

Measure What You've Done: Metrics for Growth

You can't manage what you don't measure. Whether it's revenue, customer engagement, or time spent on tasks, tracking your progress is essential for growth. Set clear metrics that will allow you to evaluate whether you're on the right path.

Tracking doesn't just show where you've succeeded—it also highlights areas that need improvement. It's easy to get discouraged if you're not seeing instant results, but consistent measurement will show you that even small progress adds up over time.

PRO TIP: Set up weekly or monthly reviews to track key performance indicators (KPIs). These could be financial (e.g., revenue growth), operational (e.g., tasks completed), or personal (e.g., hours worked without burnout). Adjust your roadmap accordingly based on what the data reveals.

CASE STUDY: JAYSON TURNS AMBITION INTO ACTION

Jayson is an aspiring entrepreneur based in Singapore. He's passionate about launching his own e-commerce platform, but like many business owners in the early stages, he's facing a unique set of challenges. His wife works full time at a multinational corporation, and as a result, Jayson is responsible for handling the bulk of child-related tasks, including dropping off and picking up their two young children from daycare. Between the demands of family life and the pressures of building a business, Jayson feels stretched thin.

However, by applying key strategies for turning ambition into action, Jayson has managed to balance his personal obligations and professional aspirations.

Morning Routine: Setting the Tone for the Day

Every morning, Jayson wakes up at 6:00 AM, not because he's naturally an early riser but because he knows that these quiet hours are the only time he has for uninterrupted work. His day starts with a quick glance at his Trello board, where he organizes every aspect of his business. He has set up separate boards for long-term projects, immediate tasks, and even his personal life. Each morning, he prioritizes the tasks he needs to accomplish that day.

Jayson's business revolves around selling eco-friendly household products, and his goal is to create a strong online presence by the end of the year. His Trello board breaks down this larger goal into manageable daily and weekly tasks, such as product listings, social media content creation, and outreach to potential suppliers.

After reviewing his tasks, Jayson blocks out his day on his calendar. Time management is crucial for him—especially with his role as the primary caregiver during the day. He knows that without a strict schedule, it's easy to fall behind. His calendar not only tracks business-related tasks but also personal commitments like dropping the kids off at daycare and family dinners.

7:00 AM: Family First, Business Second

By 7:00 AM, the kids are awake, and Jayson shifts gears into dad mode. He prepares breakfast, helps them get dressed, and makes sure they're ready for the day. By 8:30 AM, he's out the door, dropping the kids off at daycare. This part of his routine might seem unrelated to building a business, but Jayson understands that these family commitments need to be treated with the same importance as his professional goals. That's why his calendar reflects both.

By 9:00 AM, Jayson was back home and ready to start his workday. Because he's blocked off the next three hours for deep work, he knows exactly what needs to be done. His Trello board highlights the most important tasks:

contacting a new supplier in Vietnam and drafting content for his business's social media platforms. Jayson is highly aware of how valuable this uninterrupted time is, so he eliminates distractions—no phone calls, no checking emails until his most important tasks are complete.

Self-Management: Focused Work Amidst Family Responsibilities

Jayson finds self-management one of the toughest parts of running a business. When he was employed at a tech company, managing a team was straightforward—delegating tasks, ensuring deadlines were met, and overseeing projects. But now, with no one to answer to but himself, he struggles to stay on task, especially when there's laundry to fold or errands to run.

To combat this, Jayson has implemented a self-management strategy where he acts as both the CEO and the employee of his business. His Trello board holds him accountable, and he treats it like a team management tool—every task has a deadline, and he checks in with himself at the end of each week to see what he's accomplished. It might sound extreme, but by separating himself from the role of "just the founder" and approaching his tasks as a "team member," he's able to keep moving forward.

By noon, Jayson has completed his top priority tasks and spends the next 30 minutes reviewing emails and setting up meetings for the week. He uses time blocking on his calendar to ensure that these administrative tasks don't eat into his productive time.

Time Management: Maximizing the Midday Break

At 12:30 PM, Jayson takes a scheduled break. Like many entrepreneurs, he used to fall into the trap of working through meals or skipping breaks, but he quickly realized that burnout was inevitable without proper rest. He uses his calendar not just to block out time for work, but also for breaks and family commitments. If it's not scheduled, it doesn't happen.

After lunch, Jayson shifts to less demanding tasks like preparing content for his social media channels. He knows that he's not at his most creative in the afternoons, so he saves this time for tasks that require less mental energy. He spends about an hour editing photos, drafting captions, and scheduling posts using his content management tool. This ensures that his brand stays visible, even when he's focused on other parts of his business.

Afternoon: Balancing Work and Family Life

At 3:00 PM, Jayson has to pick up the kids from daycare. This is where many entrepreneurs struggle, but Jayson embraces it. By blocking off this time in his calendar, he has already mentally prepared for the shift in his day. From 3:30 PM to 5:00 PM, Jayson is in full dad mode—taking the kids to the park, helping with their homework, and making dinner. He has learned that by giving his family the same level of attention and dedication as his business, he creates balance.

Evening: Measuring Progress and Planning for Tomorrow

By 8:00 PM, after the kids are in bed, Jayson sits down for his evening review. This is when he focuses on measuring progress. Did he accomplish what he set out to do today? What are his key performance indicators (KPIs)? For Jayson, these include sales figures, website traffic, and the number of new contacts made. He checks his progress against the goals he set on his Trello board and adjusts his calendar and tasks for the rest of the week accordingly.

Jayson understands that without measurable outcomes, it's easy to lose track of growth. That's why he sets both short-term and long-term milestones and tracks them diligently. He's not just focused on how much he accomplished today—he's looking at how today's work contributes to the growth of his business over the next six months.

Conclusion: Discipline, Structure, and Accountability

Jayson's day-to-day life is a balancing act between building his business and being present for his family. By embracing strategies like self-management, time blocking, and measurable progress, he's able to stay on top of his business goals while fulfilling his family responsibilities. His story illustrates how discipline, structure, and accountability can turn ambition into action, even in the face of competing demands.

Applying the Rules: Jayson's Entrepreneurial Journey

Jayson's case study provides an excellent example of how an expat entrepreneur can apply the key principles of Discipline, Self-Management, Time Management, and Measuring Progress. Let's examine how Jayson implements each of these rules in his daily routine:

Discipline: Your Foundation for Success

Jayson demonstrates strong discipline in several ways:

- **Consistent Early Rising**: Jayson wakes up at 6:00 AM every day, not because he's naturally an early riser, but because he recognizes these quiet hours as crucial for uninterrupted work.

- **Daily Task Commitment**: He starts each day by reviewing his Trello board and prioritizing tasks, ensuring he tackles important work consistently.

- **Maintaining Routines**: Despite the challenges of balancing family responsibilities with business building, Jayson sticks to his routines, including his morning work session and evening review.

PRO TIP Application: Jayson effectively breaks down his goals into manageable tasks on his Trello board, committing to completing prioritized tasks each day.

Self-Management: Lead Yourself First

Jayson excels at self-management:

- **Dual Role Approach**: He implements a self-management strategy where he acts as both the CEO and the employee of his business.

- **Accountability System**: Jayson uses his Trello board as a team management tool, setting deadlines for tasks and checking in with himself weekly.

- **Regular Self-Evaluation**: His evening review sessions serve as "check-ins" where he reflects on his accomplishments and adjusts his plans.

PRO TIP Application: Jayson uses Trello, a project management tool, to track his daily, weekly, and monthly goals, regularly reviewing his progress.

Time Management: Maximize Your Most Valuable Resource

Jayson's approach to time management is exemplary:

- **Time Blocking**: He uses his calendar to block out time for specific tasks, including work, family commitments, and even breaks.

- **Prioritization**: Jayson schedules his most demanding tasks during his peak productivity hours in the morning.

- **Efficiency Focus**: He allocates specific time slots for different tasks, such as deep work in the morning and less demanding tasks like social media content creation in the afternoon.

PRO TIP Application: Jayson has identified his peak productivity hours (morning) and structures his most important tasks around this time for maximum efficiency.

Measure What You've Done: Metrics for Growth

Jayson demonstrates a firm commitment to measuring his progress:

- **Key Performance Indicators**: He has established clear KPIs, including sales figures, website traffic, and the number of new contacts made.

- **Regular Reviews**: Jayson conducts daily evening reviews to check his progress against set goals.

- **Adaptive Planning**: Based on his measured outcomes, Jayson adjusts his calendar and tasks for the rest of the week.

PRO TIP APPLICATION: Jayson has set up daily reviews to track his KPIs, using this data to adjust his roadmap and strategies accordingly.

By implementing these four key principles, Jayson has created a structured approach to turning his entrepreneurial ambitions into concrete actions. His methods demonstrate how discipline, effective self-management, efficient time use, and consistent progress measurement can help an expat entrepreneur balance personal responsibilities with business growth, even in a new and challenging environment.

Reflection Questions:

Take some time to reflect on how these principles apply to your own entrepreneurial journey. Weigh the following points, allowing yourself to explore your thoughts and feelings honestly. Consider journaling your thoughts or discussing them with a mentor or fellow entrepreneur. Remember, the goal is not just to think about these points, but to use your reflections to inform and inspire your actions moving forward.

Remember, self-awareness is a powerful tool for growth and success.

- Think about your current daily routine. How does it support or hinder your entrepreneurial goals? Reflect on one habit you could introduce or modify that would significantly impact your progress. What has prevented you from implementing this habit before, and how can you overcome those obstacles now?

- Consider how you currently hold yourself accountable for your goals and tasks. Are you as diligent with yourself as you would be with an employee or team member? Reflect on a recent instance where you fell short of your own expectations. How could you have managed yourself better in that situation? What systems or strategies could you implement to enhance your self-accountability?

- Think about the cultural differences or logistical issues that impact your time management. What strategies have you found effective in navigating these challenges? Are there any local customs or practices you could adopt to enhance your time management?

- Reflect on how you currently track your progress towards your goals. Are your metrics providing you with meaningful insights? Think about a recent decision you made based on the data you tracked. How did it impact your business? Are there areas of your business or personal development that you should measure but currently aren't? How could implementing new measurements in these areas benefit your entrepreneurial journey?

Action Steps:

Now it's time to put that knowledge into action. Remember, every journey begins with a single step, and by completing these actions, you're already moving forward on your path to entrepreneurial success.

Apply these principles in your daily life with the following actionable steps:

1. Establish a Morning Discipline Ritual

Action: Create a 30-minute morning routine that you'll follow every day for the next week.

How to do it:

- Choose a consistent wake-up time
- Plan 2-3 activities to include (e.g., reviewing goals, light exercise, meditation)
- Write down your routine and post it where you'll see it first thing in the morning
- Track your adherence daily

Completion: At the end of the week, review your tracking. If you've stuck to your routine for at least five out of seven days, you've successfully completed this step!

2. Implement a Personal Kanban Board

Action: Set up a personal Kanban board (physical or digital) to manage your tasks for the next five days.

How to do it:

- Choose a tool (e.g., Trello, a whiteboard, or sticky notes on a wall)
- Create three columns: "To Do," "Doing," and "Done"
- Add at least 3 tasks to your "To Do" column each day
- Move tasks across the board as you work on and complete them

Completion: If you've successfully moved at least fifteen tasks to the "Done" column by the end of the five days, you've achieved this step!

3. Practice Time Blocking for a Day

Action: Use time blocking to plan and execute your activities for one entire day.

How to do it:

- The night before, divide your waking hours into 30-minute or 1-hour blocks
- Assign a specific activity to each block, including work tasks, breaks, and personal time
- Try to stick to your schedule throughout the day
- At the end of the day, reflect on what worked and what didn't

Completion: If you've followed your time-blocked schedule for at least 80% of your day, consider this step accomplished!

4. Conduct a Weekly Measurement and Review Session

Action: At the end of your week, conduct a 30-minute review session to measure your progress.

How to do it:

- Choose 3-5 key performance indicators (KPIs) relevant to your goals
- Gather data on these KPIs (e.g., tasks completed, hours worked, progress towards a specific goal)
- Review your achievements and identify areas for improvement
- Set 2-3 specific goals for the coming week based on your review

Completion: If you've conducted your review, analyzed your KPIs, and set new goals for the upcoming week, you've successfully completed this step!

Remember, the key to these actions is consistency. Even if you don't execute them perfectly, the act of trying and reflecting on the process will provide valuable insights and help you build stronger habits over time.

Conclusion

Time management is a crucial skill, particularly when navigating the complexities of a new culture and business landscape. As you move forward, remember that turning ambition into action is an ongoing process. It requires patience, persistence, and a willingness to adapt. Embrace the challenges as opportunities for growth, and celebrate each small victory along the way.

Now that you've learned how to transform your entrepreneurial ambitions into concrete actions, it's time to shift our focus to the bigger picture. In the next part of this book, we'll explore strategies for long-term growth and sustainability in your expat-led business.

PART III

The Essentials for Global Success

CHAPTER 8

Start Now, Not Later

"If you wait for perfect conditions, you'll never get anything done."

–Ecclesiastes 11:4

"So, you're really going to do this? Now? In the middle of... everything?"

My husband's voice carried a mix of disbelief and concern as he gestured vaguely at the half-packed boxes scattered around our Dubai apartment. I looked up from my laptop, where I'd been staring at a blank document titled "Business Plan" for the past hour, the cursor blinking accusingly at me.

"I... I don't know," I admitted, running a hand through my hair. The weight of indecision pressed down on me, making the spacious bedroom feel suddenly claustrophobic. "Is there ever really a right time?"

He sighed, crossing the room to sit beside me on our bed. The mattress dipped under his weight, and I felt the warmth of his presence against my side. It was a familiar comfort, one that had seen us through countless moves and life changes over the years.

"Hun, Sennie just turned three, and the boys will be applying to college in a couple of years, and my job situation in China is still up in the air. Not to mention we're in the middle of a global pandemic. If there's a wrong time to start a business, this might be it."

I closed my eyes, feeling the weight of his words. He wasn't saying anything I hadn't already thought a hundred times over. The faces of our children flashed through my mind: Sennie, our little whirlwind of a toddler, Jovana, a budding artist always wanting to take dance and art classes; and the boys, on the cusp of adulthood, their futures stretching out before them. The responsibility I felt towards them was immense, a constant presence in every decision we made.

And yet...

"But what if it's not?" I opened my eyes, turning to face him. "What if this chaos is exactly why it's the right time?"

The warm Singapore evening air wafted through the open balcony doors, carrying with it the faint sounds of the water waves. Exotic birds called in the distance, and the chirps of lizards sporadically chimed in, reminding me of how far we were from where we'd started. In that moment, our bedroom felt both expansive with possibility and constricting with the magnitude of the decision before us.

"Think about it," I continued, my voice gaining strength as I spoke. "Every move we've made, every big decision, it's always been because of some corporation. Someone else's plans. We've been at the mercy of corporate transfers and visa regulations for years. Aren't you tired of that?" *I knew I was.*

He was quiet for a moment, his brow furrowed in thought. I could almost see the gears turning in his mind, weighing the pros and cons, as he always did. It was one thing I loved about him, his ability to be the steady, rational counterpoint to my more impulsive nature.

"Of course I am," he finally said, his voice soft. "But starting a business... that's a gigantic risk, especially now. We've always had the safety net of a corporate job. Health insurance, steady paycheck, housing allowance. Are we ready to give all that up?"

I nodded, feeling a familiar twist of anxiety in my stomach. The practical considerations he raised were valid, and they'd been haunting my thoughts for weeks. *I know. God, I know.* And that's what's been keeping me up at night, the responsibility we have to the kids, the financial implications, the sheer uncertainty of it all.

I stood up, suddenly feeling restless, and paced the room. My bare feet sank into the plush carpet with each step, grounding me as my thoughts raced. "But then I think about the girls growing up, seeing their mom chase her dreams. And the boys, learning that it's never too late to take a chance on yourself. What kind of example are we setting if we always play it too safe?"

My husband watched me, his eyes following my movement. I could see a mix of emotions playing across his face–lots of concern, understanding, and maybe a hint of excitement.

"Don't you want to be the ones making the decisions?" I asked, my words coming faster now. "To create a life where we can live and work anywhere in the world, on our own terms? We've talked about this for years, dreaming about it during our night walks. Maybe it's time we stop dreaming and start doing."

He stood up and walked over to me, placing his hands on my shoulders. His touch was steady, grounding, a reminder of the partnership that had carried us through so many adventures and challenges.

"You've always been the risk-taker between us," he said softly, a smile tugging at the corners of his mouth. "It's one thing I love about you. But it also terrifies me sometimes. You know that, right?"

I leaned into him, feeling the steady rise and fall of his chest. The familiar scent of his cologne wrapped around me, comforting and familiar amidst all the uncertainty. "I'm scared too," I whispered, voicing the fear I'd been trying to ignore. "Terrified, actually. But I'm more scared of looking back years from now and wondering 'what if?' What if we had taken the chance? What if we had believed in ourselves enough to try?"

He pulled back slightly, looking into my eyes. There was a moment of silence, heavy with the weight of the decision before us. I could see him processing, considering, his analytical mind working through scenarios.

"Tell me more about this business idea," he said finally. "What exactly are you envisioning?"

I took a deep breath, feeling a surge of excitement despite my nerves. "It's legal consulting for tech startups. I can even offer data privacy and data protection compliance. And of course, Web3 is emerging. I could add lots of value to that space."

As I spoke, I could see a spark of interest igniting in his eyes. He'd always been my sounding board, my first and most trusted advisor in all things.

"And you think now is the time to launch this? In the middle of a global pandemic when international travel is at a standstill?"

I nodded, feeling more confident with each passing moment. "That's exactly why it's the perfect time. People are facing unprecedented challenges right now. And Web3 offers people a chance to build community, and discover new ways to build businesses."

He was quiet for a moment, considering. Then, slowly, a smile spread across his face. "You know what? Maybe you're right. Everything's changing anyway, so why not change it on our terms?"

I felt a surge of excitement, tempered with a healthy dose of terror. "So... you're saying..."

He shrugged, a mix of resignation and excitement in his eyes. "I'm saying, if we're going to take a leap, we might as well do it when we're already in mid-air. We've never been ones to shy away from a challenge, have we?"

In that moment, standing in our Dubai apartment with the city humming below us and our future stretching out before us, uncertain but full of possibility, I felt a surge of clarity. The path ahead was far from clear, but for the first time in a long time, it felt like ours to choose.

I wrapped my arms around him, feeling a wave of gratitude for his support, his willingness to take this risk with me. "Thank you," I whispered. "For believing in me, in us."

He hugged me back tightly. "Always. We're in this together, remember? Through every move, every challenge, every new beginning."

As we stood there, the reality of what we were about to do sank in. There would be countless details to figure out, obstacles to overcome, moments of doubt to push through. But in that moment, all I felt was a sense of possibility.

There would never be a perfect time. There would always be reasons to wait, to play it safe. But life doesn't wait for perfect conditions. Sometimes, you have to create your own perfect storm and learn to dance in the rain.

And as I looked out over the twinkling lights of Singapore, a city-state built on ambition and dreams in the middle of the desert, I knew that's exactly what we were about to do.

Rule: Don't Look for the Perfect Moment, Look for the Perfect Storm

How many times have you heard, or perhaps told yourself, "I'll start my business when the time is right"? It's a comforting thought, isn't it? That somewhere in the future, all the stars will align, creating the perfect conditions for you to pursue your entrepreneurial dreams.

But here's the hard truth: that perfect moment is a myth.

In my years of experience as both an entrepreneur and a mentor to aspiring business owners, I've seen countless brilliant ideas wither on the vine as their creators waited for that elusive "right time." They wait for their kids to be older, for their savings account to be fuller, for the market conditions to be just right, for their current job to be less demanding. They wait, and wait, and wait... and often, they never start at all.

This mindset, while understandable, is one of the biggest obstacles holding aspiring entrepreneurs back. It's rooted in a fundamental misunderstanding of how successful businesses are born and how real entrepreneurs operate.

There is never a perfect time to start a business. There will always be challenges, always be risks, always be reasons to hesitate. Successful entrepreneurs aren't the ones who wait for perfect conditions–they're the ones who learn to thrive in imperfect ones.

This is where the concept of the Chaos Catalyst comes in.

What is a Chaos Catalyst?

A Chaos Catalyst is a moment of disruption or uncertainty that, rather than hindering your entrepreneurial journey, actually propels it forward. It's the recognition that times of change and upheaval, while challenging, are also ripe with opportunity for those willing to seize it.

Think of it like this: in chemistry, a catalyst is a substance that increases the rate of a chemical reaction without itself undergoing any permanent chemical change. Similarly, a Chaos Catalyst is an event or situation that speeds up your entrepreneurial journey without altering your core vision or values.

How chaos and uncertainty can spark innovation and opportunity

Chaos and uncertainty, while often feared, are actually powerful drivers of innovation and opportunity. Why? Because disruption creates gaps in the market, shifts consumer needs, and renders old solutions obsolete. For the alert and agile entrepreneur, these are all openings to create value.

Consider how some of the most successful companies of our time were born out of periods of chaos:

1. **Problem-solving in crisis**: When faced with unprecedented challenges, people, and businesses are more open to new solutions. This creates a fertile ground for innovative products and services.

2. **Shifting priorities**: Times of upheaval often lead to a re-evaluation of what's truly important. This can open up new markets or increase demand in certain sectors.

3. **Resource reallocation**: Economic shifts can free up talent, technology, or other resources that can be leveraged by savvy entrepreneurs.

4. **Accelerated adoption of new technologies**: Crises often force rapid adaptation, leading to faster adoption of new technologies and ways of doing business.

Historical examples of businesses born in turbulent times

History is filled with examples of successful businesses that were born in the midst of chaos:

- **General Electric**: Founded in 1892 during an economic depression, GE became one of the largest and most diversified technology and manufacturing companies in the world.

- **Microsoft**: Started during the oil embargo and stock market crash of 1973-1975, Microsoft capitalized on the personal computer revolution to become a tech giant.

- **Airbnb**: Founded in 2008 during the Financial Crisis, Airbnb provided a way for people to earn extra income by renting out spare rooms, eventually disrupting the entire hospitality industry.

- **Square**: Also founded during the 2009 recession, Square provided an easy way for small businesses to accept credit card payments, filling a crucial need during tough economic times.

These companies didn't succeed despite the chaotic times they were born in, in many ways, they succeeded because of them. They identified needs that arose from the upheaval around them and created innovative solutions to meet those needs.

The Chaos Catalyst, then, is about more than just timing. It's a mindset—a way of viewing disruption not as an obstacle, but as an opportunity. It's about having the courage to act when others are paralyzed by uncertainty, and the vision to see possibilities where others see only problems.

In the following sections, we'll explore how you can cultivate this mindset and leverage your own Chaos Catalysts to fuel your entrepreneurial journey. But first, let's return to that moment in my Singapore apartment, where my own Chaos Catalyst was about to ignite.

Recognizing Catalytic Moments in Your Life

As I stood in that Singapore apartment, surrounded by half-packed boxes and uncertainty, I was face-to-face with my own Chaos Catalyst. But how do you recognize these pivotal moments in your own life? Let's explore some common catalytic moments that could spark your entrepreneurial journey.

Personal transitions

Life is full of transitions, and each one carries the potential to be a Chaos Catalyst:

- **Career changes**: Whether it's a layoff, a promotion, or a career pivot, changes in your professional life can open up new perspectives and opportunities.

- **Moves**: Relocating, especially internationally, exposes you to new markets, cultures, and ways of thinking. Our move to Singapore, for instance, opened my eyes to the unique challenges faced by expats and international businesses.

- **Family changes**: Major life events like marriage, divorce, or having children can shift your priorities and inspire new business ideas.

Remember, my decision to start a legal consulting business for tech startups didn't happen in a vacuum. It was the culmination of years of international moves, career experiences, and personal growth—all catalytic moments in their own right.

Market disruptions and shifts

Keep an eye on broader economic and industry trends:

- **Technological advancements**: The rise of new technologies often creates gaps in the market. Think of how smartphones created opportunities for app developers, or how blockchain is opening up new possibilities in finance and beyond.

- **Regulatory changes**: New laws or regulations can create demand for compliance solutions or open up previously restricted markets.

- **Shifts in consumer behavior**: Changes in how people live, work, and consume can reveal unmet needs. The rise of remote work, for example, has created opportunities in everything from home office equipment to virtual team-building services.

Global events and crises

While often challenging, global events can be powerful Chaos Catalysts:

- **Economic recessions**: Downturns can create opportunities for more efficient, cost-effective solutions.

- **Health crises**: The COVID-19 pandemic, for instance, accelerated trends in remote work, e-commerce, and telemedicine.

- **Environmental challenges**: Climate change is driving innovation in sustainable technologies and practices.

- **Geopolitical shifts**: Changes in international relations can open up new markets or create a demand for cross-cultural services.

The key is to train yourself to see these moments not as obstacles, but as potential launch pads for your entrepreneurial dreams.

The Psychology of Embracing Chaos

Recognizing catalytic moments is one thing; embracing them is another. Let's explore the mindset shifts necessary to become a true Chaos Catalyst entrepreneur.

Overcoming fear and resistance to change

Fear is a natural response to uncertainty, but it doesn't have to paralyze you:

- **Acknowledge your fears**: Name them, write them down. Often, bringing fears into the light makes them less daunting.

- **Reframe risk**: Instead of focusing on what you might lose, consider what you might gain, or what you might lose by not acting.

- **Start small**: You don't have to quit your job and bet everything on a new venture immediately. Start with small experiments to build confidence.

In my own journey, I grappled with fears about financial security and the impact on my family. But by facing these fears head-on and discussing them openly with my husband, we were able to develop a plan that felt both exciting and responsible.

Developing a Growth Mindset in Uncertain Times

A growth mindset–the belief that your abilities can be developed through dedication and hard work–is crucial for Chaos Catalyst entrepreneurs:

- **Embrace challenges**: See them as opportunities to learn and grow, not as threats.

- **Learn from criticism**: Feedback, even negative feedback, can be a valuable tool for improvement.

- **Find inspiration in others' success**: Instead of feeling threatened by others' achievements, let them inspire you.

- **Emphasize learning over failure**: If something doesn't work out, ask yourself, "What can I learn from this?" rather than "Why did I fail?"

Building Resilience and Adaptability

Resilience, the ability to bounce back from setbacks, and adaptability, the ability to adjust to new conditions, are key traits of successful entrepreneurs:

1. **Cultivate a support network**: Surround yourself with people who believe in you and can offer emotional and practical support.

2. **Practice self-care**: Maintain your physical and mental health. You can't navigate chaos if you're running on empty.

3. **Stay curious**: Continuously learn and explore. The more knowledge and skills you have, the more adaptable you'll be.

4. **Embrace imperfection**: Don't let the pursuit of perfection hold you back. Remember, in chaotic times, done is often better than perfect.

CASE STUDY: DAMIEN'S JOURNEY FROM TRAILING SPOUSE TO ENTREPRENEURIAL ARCHITECT

Damien stood at the window of their new London flat, watching the rain create intricate patterns on the glass. The gray sky seemed to mirror his mood–uncertain, a bit gloomy, but with hints of brightness breaking through.

"Hey, how's the view?" Cheryl's voice broke through his reverie. She wrapped her arms around him from behind, resting her chin on his shoulder.

Damien managed a small smile. "It's... different. Lots of brick and narrow streets. Nothing like Chicago."

"I know this is a big change," Cheryl said softly. "But it's going to be an amazing opportunity for us. For both of us."

Damien turned to face her, his expression a mix of love and apprehension. "I know, I know. And I'm excited for you, truly. This role at the consulting firm is huge. It's just..."

"Just what?" Cheryl prompted gently.

"I feel... lost," Damien admitted. "Back home, I had my job at the firm, my clients, my routine. Here, I'm just... what? The trailing spouse?"

Cheryl's face fell slightly. "You're so much more than that, and you know it. You're a brilliant architect, Damien. This could be your chance to do something different, something you've always wanted."

Damien sighed, running a hand through his hair. "Maybe. But who's going to hire an American architect who doesn't know the first thing about British building codes or planning permissions?"

"Then don't get hired," Cheryl said, a spark lighting up her eyes. "Start your own firm. Isn't that what you've always dreamed of?"

Damien let out a short laugh. "Right, because starting a business in a foreign country during a global economic downturn is such a great idea."

"Why not?" Cheryl challenged. "Think about it. You've always talked about wanting to focus on sustainable, eco-friendly designs. London is at the forefront of green architecture. This could be your moment."

Damien paused, considering her words. For the first time since they'd arrived in London two weeks ago, he felt a small flicker of excitement.

The next few months were a whirlwind of activity. Damien threw himself into researching the London architecture scene, British regulations, and the latest trends in sustainable design. He networked tirelessly, attending every industry event he could find.

One rainy evening (as many London evenings were), Damien burst into their flat, his eyes alight with excitement.

"Cheryl, you won't believe what happened!" he exclaimed.

Cheryl looked up from her laptop, intrigued. "What's got you so fired up?"

"I met this developer at a green building symposium," Damien explained, shrugging off his rain-soaked coat. "He's working on this huge project to convert old industrial buildings into eco-friendly mixed-use spaces. We got talking, and... he wants me to submit a proposal!"

Cheryl's face broke into a huge grin. "Damien, that's fantastic! See? I told you your skills would be valuable here."

Damien's excitement faltered slightly. "But... I don't have a firm. I'm not even properly licensed here yet. How can I possibly take on a project this big?"

Cheryl stood up and took his hands in hers. "This is it, Damien. This is your Chaos Catalyst moment. Remember what we talked about? Sometimes the craziest times are when the biggest opportunities appear."

Damien took a deep breath, feeling a mix of terror and exhilaration. "You're right. This is crazy, but... maybe that's exactly why it could work."

Over the next few weeks, Damien worked tirelessly on his proposal. He leveraged every contact he'd made, sought advice from fellow expat entrepreneurs, and even took crash courses in British business law.

The night before his presentation to the developer, Damien sat at their dining table, surrounded by sketches and documents. Cheryl brought him a cup of tea and sat beside him.

"How are you feeling?" she asked.

Damien looked up, his eyes tired but bright. "Terrified. Excited. Like I'm standing on the edge of a cliff, about to jump off."

Cheryl smiled. "But this time, you've built your own wings."

Damien nodded, a slow smile spreading across his face. "You know, when we first came here, I felt so lost. Like I was just tagging along on your adventure. But now..."

"Now it's your adventure too," Cheryl finished for him.

"Exactly," Damien agreed. "All this chaos—the move, the new country, the economic uncertainty—it's not just a challenge. It's opportunity. My opportunity."

The next day, Damien nailed his presentation. The developer was impressed not just by his designs, but by his unique perspective as an American architect with a fresh take on London's architectural landscape.

As Damien walked out of the meeting, the proposal accepted and first project secured, he felt a profound sense of gratitude for the chaos that had brought him here. He pulled out his phone and dialed Cheryl.

"Hey," he said when she answered. "How do you feel about being married to the founder of London's newest sustainable architecture firm?"

Cheryl's joyful laugh echoed through the phone. "I'd say it's about time you embraced the chaos, Mr. Entrepreneur."

Damien grinned, looking up at the London skyline—a skyline he now saw not just as buildings, but as possibilities. "You know what? I couldn't agree more."

As he walked home through the bustling London streets, Damien reflected on his journey. From reluctant trailing spouse to excited entrepreneur, he had discovered that sometimes, the greatest opportunities arise from the most chaotic situations. All it takes is the courage to see the catalyst in the chaos.

Applying the Chaos Catalyst: Damian's Journey

Damian's story exemplifies the power of the Chaos Catalyst in action. Let's examine four key ways he embraced chaos to fuel his entrepreneurial journey:

Leveraging Career Transition

Instead of viewing his role as a "trailing spouse" as a setback, Damian used this career disruption as a catalyst for change. He saw it as an opportunity to break free from his previous job constraints and pursue his long-held dream of starting his own architecture firm. This shift in perspective transformed a potentially negative situation into a launching pad for his entrepreneurial ambitions.

Embracing Relocation as Opportunity

Damian turned the challenges of moving to a new country into advantages. Rather than being intimidated by his unfamiliarity with London, he used his fresh perspective as a unique selling point. He immersed himself in the local architecture scene, attending events and building a network from scratch. This approach to his new environment opened doors that might have remained closed if he had stayed in his comfort zone back in Chicago.

Adapting to Regulatory Changes

Instead of being deterred by his lack of knowledge about British building codes and planning permissions, Damian saw this as an opportunity for growth. He threw himself into learning about local regulations, taking crash courses in British business law. This willingness to acquire new knowledge not only prepared him for his new market but also gave him insights that set him apart from local competitors who might take these regulations for granted.

Aligning with Environmental Challenges

Damian recognized the growing emphasis on sustainable, eco-friendly designs in London's architecture scene. Rather than seeing this as just another hurdle, he positioned it as a central focus of his new firm. By aligning his expertise with this market demand, he turned a global challenge into a business opportunity. His proposal for converting old industrial buildings into eco-friendly mixed-use spaces demonstrated how he could contribute to solving environmental challenges while also establishing his business.

These four aspects of Damian's journey show how the Chaos Catalyst operates in real-life situations. By reframing disruptions as opportunities, rapidly adapting to new circumstances, and aligning his skills with emerging needs, Damian could transform a period of personal and professional upheaval into the foundation of a promising new venture. His story illustrates that the key to leveraging the Chaos Catalyst lies not in waiting for perfect conditions, but in creatively engaging with the challenges at hand.

Take a Moment to Reflect

Reflection Questions:

Now it's time to reflect on your own life and identify potential Chaos Catalysts. Consider the following questions:

1. What major changes or upheavals are you currently experiencing in your life? How might these be potential catalysts for new opportunities?

2. Think about a time when a disruption in your life led to unexpected positive outcomes. What lessons can you draw from that experience?

3. What skills or perspectives do you have that might be valuable in a new or changing context? How could you leverage these in entrepreneurial ways?

4. Are there any market trends or shifts in your industry that others might see as threatening, but which you could turn into opportunities?

5. What's the biggest fear holding you back from embracing change in your life or career? How might you reframe this fear as a potential for growth?

6. If you were to start a business right now, in the midst of your current life circumstances, what would it look like? What unique advantages might your current situation provide?

7. Who are the people in your life who could support you in embracing chaos and pursuing new opportunities? How can you engage them in your journey?

8. What small step could you take today to turn a current life challenge into a catalyst for positive change?

Remember, the Chaos Catalyst is not about recklessly diving into upheaval, but about developing the mindset to see opportunities where others see only obstacles. By reflecting on these questions, you can cultivate this mindset and prepare yourself to leverage the chaos in your own life as a catalyst for entrepreneurial success.

Action Steps:

Now that you've reflected on the concept of the Chaos Catalyst, it's time to put these ideas into practice in your own life. The following action steps help you identify, analyze, and leverage the chaos in your own circumstances. Remember, the goal isn't to create chaos, but to harness the potential within the challenges you're already facing.

To help you apply the Chaos Catalyst concept in your own life, try these three practical exercises:

1. Chaos Mapping Exercise

Take out your journal and follow these steps:

- Draw a circle on the center of a page and write "Me" inside it.
- Around this circle, draw smaller circles representing different areas of your life (e.g., career, relationships, health, finances, personal growth).
- For each area, list any current disruptions, changes, or uncertainties you're experiencing.
- Now, draw lines connecting these chaos points to potential opportunities. For example, if you're experiencing a career transition, connect

it to "chance to explore new industries" or "opportunity to start a side hustle."

- Reflect on your map. Which area of chaos seems to hold the most potential? What surprising connections did you discover?

This exercise helps you visualize the chaos in your life and start seeing it as a web of potential opportunities rather than isolated problems.

2. The "Five Whys" of Opportunity

Choose one area of chaos in your life. In your journal, ask yourself, "Why is this an opportunity?" Then, take your answer and ask "Why?" again. Repeat this process five times.

For example:

- Why is losing my job an opportunity? *Because I can explore new career paths.*

- Why is exploring new career paths an opportunity? *Because I can find work that's more fulfilling.*

- Why is finding more fulfilling work an opportunity? *Because it could lead to greater job satisfaction and performance.*

- Why is greater job satisfaction something I should seek? *Because it could improve my overall quality of life.*

- Why is improving my quality of life an opportunity? *Because it could inspire me to take on new challenges and grow in other areas of my life.*

This exercise helps you reframe chaos as an opportunity and uncover deeper insights about what you truly want.

3. Weekly Chaos Check-In

Set a recurring reminder in your calendar for a weekly "Chaos Check-In." During this time:

- Identify one new or ongoing source of chaos in your life.

- List three potential opportunities this chaos might be creating.

- Choose one small, concrete action you can take in the next week to explore or leverage one of these opportunities.

- The following week, reflect on the action you took and its results.

For example: Chaos: Unexpected work-from-home order Opportunities:

1. More time to learn new skills online

2. Chance to redesign home office for better productivity

3. Opportunity to propose remote work policy improvements to management

Conclusion: Embracing the Chaos Catalyst

As we've explored throughout this chapter, the Chaos Catalyst is more than just a concept—it's a powerful mindset that can transform the way you approach entrepreneurship and life. We've seen how disruptions, uncertainties, and challenges that might initially appear as obstacles can, with the right perspective, become the very fuel that propels us forward.

Looking at the Chaos Catalyst principle in action in Damian's journey as a trailing spouse turned entrepreneur, we've uncovered several key insights:

1. There is no "perfect" time to start a business or pursue your dreams. Often, the most chaotic times can offer unique opportunities for those willing to see them.

2. Personal transitions, market disruptions, and global events, while challenging, can all serve as catalysts for innovation and growth.

3. Embracing chaos requires a shift in mindset—from seeing disruption as a threat to viewing it as a potential launching pad for new ventures.

4. Successful entrepreneurs don't wait for ideal conditions; they learn to thrive amidst uncertainty by being adaptable, resilient, and open to new possibilities.

5. The Chaos Catalyst approach isn't about recklessly diving into upheaval, but about developing the skills to identify and leverage opportunities within challenging circumstances.

As you move forward from this chapter, remember that chaos is not something to be feared or avoided, but a force that can be harnessed. By applying the action steps and continually practicing the Chaos Catalyst mindset, you'll be better equipped to navigate the unpredictable waters of entrepreneurship.

Your journey as an entrepreneur will inevitably involve moments of uncertainty and disruption. But armed with the Chaos Catalyst perspective, you're now prepared to see these moments not as setbacks, but as potential turning points—the sparks that could ignite your next great idea or propel your business to new heights.

Embrace the chaos, seek the opportunities within it, and let it catalyze your entrepreneurial success. The next chapter of your business story is waiting to be written—and it might just start with the very chaos you're facing right now.

CHAPTER 9

The Tech You Need

"The first rule of any technology used in a business is that automation applied to an efficient operation will magnify the efficiency."

–Bill Gates

I was up late, tired and annoyed, with my laptop clock showing 12:37 AM and another error message. My fingers the maze of braids in my hair as I let out a moan of exhaustion. This wasn't how I'd imagined spending my nights when I dreamed up ByteBao's new offering, a Web3 education platform for lawyers.

"You're a tech lawyer," I muttered to myself. "You should be able to handle this." But as I looked at the tangle of open tabs—each one a different video editing software trial—I felt a familiar wave of doubt wash over me.

Fresh out of my cushy bank job and armed with a vision of bridging the gap between law and the burgeoning world of Web3, I'd naively thought my tech-savviness would be enough. How wrong I was.

The first wake-up call came when I tried to set up the website and learning management system. I'd confidently signed up for a popular platform, only to find myself lost in a maze of settings and integrations three days later. As I stared at the mess of a homepage I'd created, a realization hit me: I wasn't just building a business; I was embarking on a crash course in modern technology.

Determined to get it right, I threw myself into research. I spent weeks comparing platforms, watching tutorials, and pestering more tech-savvy friends for advice. My dining table disappeared under a sea of notepads filled with scribbled features, pros, and cons of each system. I even dreamed in dropdown menus and toggle switches.

Finally, after what felt like a hundred demos, I found a solution that worked—or so I thought. The day I launched the ByteBao website, I felt on top of the world. I worked with a freelance designer to create a sleek interface and intuitive navigation. After we finished, I celebrated with a glass of wine, thinking the troublesome part was done.

Two months and a growing user base later, reality struck again. As I was processing our first batch of course payments, I discovered our payment processing system wouldn't integrate smoothly with our chosen platform. What should have been a moment of triumph turned into a nightmare of error messages and failed transactions.

Cue another round of late nights and frantic learning. I dove into the world of payment gateways and API integrations, terms that had seemed abstract in my tech law days but now took on urgent, practical meaning. After a week of trials and troubleshooting, I finally got the systems to play nice. But the experience left me with a newfound respect for the complexities lurking beneath even the simplest online transactions.

But nothing prepared me for the video editing saga. As demand for our Web3 courses grew, so did the need for engaging video content. "How hard can it be?" I thought, as I downloaded a trial of Adobe Premiere Pro.

Three days later, I was ready to throw my laptop out the window. The software was powerful, sure, but it felt like trying to crack a safe with a sledgehammer. Every simple task seemed to require navigating through layers of menus and options. And when I finally figured out how to add a simple text overlay, the preview crashed, losing an hour's work.

Worse, the monthly subscription fee made my eyes water. As a bootstrapped start-up, every dollar counted, and the Adobe suite felt like a luxury we couldn't afford.

So began the great video editor hunt of 2023. I tried free tools that crashed every other export, leaving me with half-rendered videos and frayed nerves. I experimented with mid-range options that looked like they were designed in the 90s, their clunky interfaces a far cry from the sleek Web3 image I wanted for ByteBao.

With each new software, I had to learn a new interface, new shortcuts, new quirks. It was maddening. One week, I'd feel like I was finally getting the hang of a program, only to discover it couldn't handle the type of animations I needed for explaining blockchain concepts.

And yet, with each failure, each frustrating night, I was learning. Not just about video editing, but about the process of finding the right tools for ByteBao. I was learning to balance functionality with cost, to weigh the benefits of powerful features against the reality of our tight startup budget.

I was also learning about myself—about my capacity to adapt, to push through frustration, to find creative solutions. Each obstacle was a chance to prove that I could be more than just a lawyer who understood tech; I could be an entrepreneur who wielded it.

Finally, after what felt like my hundredth software download, I found DaVinci Resolve. It wasn't perfect, but it was powerful enough for our needs, intuitive enough for me to learn quickly, and—best of all—it had a robust, free version. As I successfully exported our first course video at 3 AM, I felt a surge of triumph that made all the struggles worth it.

But the challenges didn't stop there. Just as I thought I had our tech stack figured out, the rug was pulled out from under me again. Six months into using our project management software—a tool our entire team had finally gotten comfortable with—a new player entered the market.

The new software promised all the features we loved, plus innovative tools that seemed tailor-made for our needs, all at half the price we were currently paying. It was tempting, but I hesitated. I thought about the hours we'd spent setting up our current system, the team's familiarity with it, the data we'd accumulated.

"If it ain't broke, don't fix it," a voice in my head argued. But another voice, one that had grown stronger through this journey, countered, "But what if it could be better?"

After days of deliberation and number-crunching, we took the plunge. The transition was rough. We lost some data in the migration, and my team's frustration was palpable as they grappled with the new interface. For a few weeks, I second-guessed my decision constantly.

But slowly, things improved. The new features streamlined our workflows in ways we hadn't anticipated. The cost savings allowed us to invest in better equipment for video production. As I watched our productivity and content quality improve, I realized that this constant evolution—this willingness to embrace change and weather the storm of transition—was part of the journey.

Now, a year into ByteBao's life, as I close my laptop after a surprisingly smooth editing session, I can't help but chuckle at how far I've come. The tech landscape is still daunting, still ever-changing. But I've learned to surf its waves rather than being overwhelmed by them.

Every new tool, every system update, every shiny new software that enters the market is both a challenge and an opportunity. Sometimes it pays to jump on board; other times, it's wiser to stay the course. The trick, I've learned, is to never stop learning, never stop evaluating, and never be afraid to admit when it's time for a change.

As I head to bed, my mind is already buzzing with ideas for our next course module. I know there will be more late nights, more frustrations, more moments of doubt. But I also know that with each challenge, ByteBao—and I—will emerge stronger, more adaptable, and better equipped to navigate the ever-evolving maze of technology that shapes our digital world.

In the end, isn't that what entrepreneurship is all about? It's not just about having a great idea or understanding your field. It's about being willing to dive into the unknown, to grapple with new challenges, and to reinvent yourself.

As I drift off to sleep, I smile, thinking about how my journey with ByteBao has transformed me. From a tech lawyer who thought she knew it all, to an entrepreneur humbled by technology, to someone who now sees each tech challenge as an exciting puzzle to solve. It's been a wild ride, and it's only just beginning.

Tomorrow brings new challenges: AI integration, blockchain updates, maybe even venturing into virtual reality for our courses. But now, instead of dread, I feel a spark of excitement. Because I know that with each technological hurdle we overcome, we're not just improving ByteBao—we're helping to shape the future of legal education in the Web3 era.

And that, despite all the late nights and frustrations, makes it all worthwhile.

Rule: Use the S.M.A.R.T. Path to Tech Success

Starting a business involves overcoming several challenges, but navigating the technology landscape is one of the most critical. Technology can either propel your business forward or create stumbling blocks if not handled effectively. The S.M.A.R.T. Path to Tech Success outlines five key principles to help entrepreneurs leverage technology efficiently while avoiding common pitfalls. Let's explore each principle in depth.

1. Set Up Your Tech Knowledge Early

Technology is the backbone of nearly every successful business today, yet many entrepreneurs feel overwhelmed by the array of digital tools and platforms they must understand. The key to overcoming this challenge is to start small and build your knowledge over time. Instead of trying to become an expert in all things tech, focus on the fundamentals that directly impact your business. Learn how customer relationship management (CRM) systems streamline sales processes, explore e-commerce platforms to understand their features, and familiarize yourself with social media's role in driving engagement and traffic.

As a business owner, you don't need to code a website or master all digital marketing techniques, but you should understand enough to make informed decisions. This foundational knowledge will help you feel more confident and empowered, enabling you to engage more effectively with technical professionals you may hire.

PRO TIP: Break down your learning into manageable chunks. Dedicate an hour each week to exploring a new digital tool relevant to your business. Consider free trials or demo versions to experiment with software without committing to paid services upfront.

2. Master Tech Adaptability

The digital landscape is constantly evolving. New tools and platforms emerge frequently, and consumer behavior shifts just as quickly. What worked for your business last year may not work tomorrow. Entrepreneurs must stay nimble and be prepared to pivot their tech strategies as needed. This doesn't mean chasing every shiny new tool on the market, but it does require being open to change and staying informed about trends in technology that could benefit your business.

For example, as automation tools and artificial intelligence (AI) evolve, many entrepreneurs are adopting these technologies to optimize customer service, streamline internal processes, and make data-driven decisions. Entrepreneurs who resist change risk falling behind their competitors. Being adaptable also means being willing to let go of outdated technology that no longer serves your business effectively.

PRO TIP: Keep a "future trends" list where you track emerging technologies that may be relevant to your industry. Set reminders every quarter to review this list and assess whether it's time to implement a new tool or upgrade an existing one.

3. Align Your Tech Stack for Growth

Your tech stack—the combination of software and digital tools that power your business—should be carefully selected with long-term growth in mind. The goal is not just to find tools that meet your current needs, but to choose platforms that can scale with your business. As you expand, your systems should handle increased customer demand, more complex operations, and greater data volumes without breaking down or requiring expensive overhauls.

For instance, if you're setting up an online store, choosing an e-commerce platform that integrates easily with your accounting software, payment systems, and inventory management tools will save you headaches later. Entrepreneurs who neglect this step often pay for multiple services that don't integrate well, leading to data inconsistencies and operational inefficiencies.

PRO TIP: When evaluating new tools, think long term. Ask yourself whether the software will still serve you when your customer base grows or when you add new services. Opt for platforms with built-in scalability, even if they are slightly more expensive upfront.

4. Refine Integration for Efficiency

Even the best tools can become a burden if they don't work well together. Integration is key to ensuring that the different parts of your tech stack communicate seamlessly, helping you avoid redundant manual work and eliminate data silos. Poor integration leads to inefficiencies, where time and effort are wasted on tasks that should be automated or simplified by software.

For example, imagine you're running a marketing campaign and generating new leads. If your email marketing tool doesn't integrate with your CRM, you'll have to manually input contact information, risking errors and slowing down the entire process. On the other hand, well-integrated tools allow data to flow freely between systems, automatically syncing customer information, sales records, and marketing data in real time.

Integration also plays a significant role in customer experience. When tools work together smoothly, customers enjoy a more personalized and seamless experience, whether it's through better-targeted emails, faster support responses, or accurate order tracking.

PRO TIP: Start small by integrating your most critical systems first, such as your CRM and email marketing tools. Use middleware solutions like Zapier or Automate.io to bridge the gap between tools that don't have native integrations. Regularly audit your processes to ensure integration continues to meet your needs.

5.   Tech-Forward Budgeting for Sustainable Growth

Technology investments are essential for any business, but they need to be balanced with sustainability in mind. Many entrepreneurs, especially in the startup phase, find themselves either overspending on the latest tools or under-investing in crucial infrastructure. Neither extreme is ideal—overspending can drain resources, while under-investing can hamper growth and leave you lagging competitors.

To create a sustainable tech budget, start by identifying the most essential tools your business needs to operate efficiently, such as a website platform, marketing tools, and payment systems. Next, factor in ongoing costs like software subscriptions, upgrades, and any future technology you may need to adopt as you scale. Don't forget about cybersecurity and backup solutions, which are critical but often overlooked in early-stage tech planning.

PRO TIP: Use the 80/20 rule when budgeting for technology—allocate 80% of your budget to tools that have an immediate impact on your business and reserve 20% for exploring new technologies that can drive future growth. This allows you to remain flexible without compromising on necessary expenses.

CASE STUDY: AN ASPIRING ENTREPRENEUR'S JOURNEY ON THE S.M.A.R.T. PATH TO TECH SUCCESS

Ethan Choi, a 48-year-old corporate lawyer, had spent his entire 25-year career at a prestigious law firm in Chicago. While he was comfortable using technology for legal research and document preparation, he had never delved deeper into the digital world. Social media was a mystery to him, and terms like "CRM" and "e-commerce platform" were outside his vocabulary.

However, Ethan had always harbored a passion for environmental law and sustainability. Inspired by the growing demand for eco-friendly products and his desire to make a bigger impact, he took the leap into entrepreneurship. His goal was to launch EcoLegal, an online platform offering legal advice and resources for sustainable businesses.

As an aspiring entrepreneur, Ethan quickly realized that his limited tech knowledge could become a significant obstacle. One evening, after spending hours trying to set up a simple website for his new venture, he slumped in his chair, running his hands through his graying hair.

"What was I thinking?" he muttered to himself. "I'm a lawyer, not a tech guru. Maybe I'm too old for this. Maybe I should just stick to what I know and forget about being an entrepreneur."

His wife, Olivia, overheard his frustration. "Ethan, you've faced tough cases before. This is just a different kind of challenge. Why don't you look for some resources to help you learn? Lots of aspiring entrepreneurs start from scratch with tech."

Encouraged by Olivia's words, Ethan began researching and soon discovered the S.M.A.R.T. Path to Tech Success. Determined to make his entrepreneurial vision a reality, he embraced this approach.

Setting Up Tech Knowledge Early

Ethan knew he needed to build a sound foundation of tech knowledge quickly if he wanted to succeed as an entrepreneur. He started by dedicating one hour each evening to learning about different aspects of running an online business. He used free resources like Coursera and YouTube to understand the basics of website development, digital marketing, and customer relationship management.

At first, the sheer volume of information overwhelmed him. "I feel like I'm drowning in a sea of tech jargon," he confessed to Olivia one night. "How am I supposed to learn all this and launch a business from scratch?"

Olivia gently reminded him, "Every successful entrepreneur started somewhere, Ethan. Take it one step at a time."

Taking her advice to heart, Ethan broke down his learning into manageable chunks. He created a weekly schedule, focusing on one aspect of technology at a time. Monday was for website basics, Tuesday for digital marketing, Wednesday for CRM, and so on.

To gain hands-on experience, Ethan signed up for free trials of various software platforms. He experimented with WordPress for website building, Mailchimp for email marketing, and HubSpot's free CRM. This approach allowed him to familiarize himself with different tools with no financial commitment—a crucial consideration for an aspiring entrepreneur with limited resources.

There were moments of triumph, like when he successfully set up his first email campaign. "Olivia! Come look at this!" he called excitedly. "I just sent a test email to myself using Mailchimp! I'm starting to feel like a real tech entrepreneur!"

But there were also moments of deep frustration. One day, after struggling for hours with WordPress, Ethan slammed his laptop shut. "This is impossible," he growled. "I'm a seasoned lawyer, for heaven's sake. How do real entrepreneurs figure out how to change a font color on a website?"

Despite these setbacks, Ethan persevered, reminding himself that every successful entrepreneur faced similar challenges. He joined online forums and local tech meetups, slowly building a network of fellow aspiring entrepreneurs he could turn to for advice. Gradually, his confidence grew.

Within two months, Ethan had a solid grasp of the digital landscape. He could now confidently discuss his tech needs with potential developers and make informed decisions about EcoLegal's digital infrastructure—a crucial skill for any modern entrepreneur.

Mastering Tech Adaptability

As Ethan delved deeper into the tech world, he realized that being adaptable was a key trait of successful entrepreneurs. He set up a "Tech Trends" document where he regularly noted emerging technologies relevant to online legal services.

When he first launched EcoLegal, Ethan relied heavily on written content. However, he soon noticed a growing trend in video consumption among successful online businesses. The thought of appearing on camera filled him with dread.

"I can't do this, Olivia," he said one evening. "I'm a lawyer, not a YouTuber. What if I make a fool of myself? No one will take me seriously as an entrepreneur."

Olivia smiled encouragingly. "Remember when you were nervous about your first court appearance? This is no different. Practice makes perfect. Plus, think about how many entrepreneurs are using video to connect with their audience."

Despite his initial discomfort, Ethan adapted, recognizing that this was part of his journey as an aspiring entrepreneur. He set up a small home studio in the spare room and started practicing. His first attempts were awkward and stilted. "Delete that immediately," he told Olivia after watching his first recording. "I look like a deer in headlights! No wonder so many people are afraid to start their own businesses."

But Ethan persisted, reminding himself that every successful entrepreneur had to start somewhere. He took an online course in public speaking and studied popular legal YouTubers. Slowly but surely, he improved. He learned basic video editing skills and started producing short, informative videos about environmental law for social media platforms.

This adaptability paid off. EcoLegal's engagement rates soared, and client acquisition costs decreased significantly. Ethan's willingness to embrace new technologies and formats helped position EcoLegal as a modern, accessible legal resource, setting him apart from other aspiring entrepreneurs in the legal tech space.

Aligning Tech Stack for Growth

With his newfound knowledge, Ethan handpicked EcoLegal's tech stack with scalability in mind. This process was not without its challenges.

"I feel like I'm playing a high-stakes game of Jenga," Ethan confided in a fellow aspiring entrepreneur at a networking event. "One wrong move in choosing these tools, and my whole business idea could come crashing down before it even takes off."

The entrepreneur laughed. "We all feel that way at first. The key is to choose tools that can grow with you. That's what separates successful startups from the ones that fizzle out."

Taking this advice to heart, Ethan chose WordPress with WooCommerce for the website and online store, knowing it could handle increased traffic and transactions as the business grew. For customer management, he opted for Salesforce, which, while more expensive than some alternatives, offered robust features that would support EcoLegal's long-term growth.

Ethan also invested in a comprehensive legal research database that could integrate with his chosen platforms. This decision wasn't easy—the cost made him break out in a cold sweat. "Are we sure about this?" he asked Olivia. "It's a lot of money for something we might not need right away. What if EcoLegal doesn't take off?"

"Think long term," Olivia reminded him. "You're building for the future, not just for today. That's what real entrepreneurs do."

This foresight proved invaluable when, eighteen months later, EcoLegal expanded to offer personalized legal document preparation. The scalable tech stack allowed for a smooth integration of this new service with no major overhauls, a flexibility that Ethan knew was crucial for a growing startup.

Refining Integration for Efficiency

As EcoLegal grew from an idea to a fledgling business, Ethan focused on refining the integration between his various tools to boost efficiency. He used Zapier to create automated workflows between Salesforce, his email marketing platform, and his scheduling software.

At first, the idea of automation made Ethan nervous. "What if something goes wrong?" he fretted. "What if we lose important client information? I'm just starting out—I can't afford to make mistakes."

To ease his concerns, Ethan started small. He began by automating just one process: when a potential client booked a consultation through the website, their information would automatically be added to Salesforce. Seeing this work flawlessly gave Ethan the confidence to expand the automation.

Soon, booking a consultation would not only add the client to Salesforce but also trigger a welcome email sequence and add the appointment to Ethan's calendar. This integration saved hours of manual data entry each week and ensured no leads fell through the cracks—a crucial efficiency for a solo entrepreneur just starting out.

Ethan also integrated his legal research database with his document preparation software. This allowed him to quickly pull relevant legal information while drafting documents for clients, significantly reducing the time required for each project.

As he watched his efficiency skyrocket, Ethan couldn't help but laugh at his former technophobia. "If only I could go back and tell myself how much easier this would make everything," he mused. "I'm starting to feel like a real tech-savvy entrepreneur!"

Tech-Forward Budgeting for Sustainable Growth

Ethan approached EcoLegal's tech budget with a long-term perspective, a strategy he knew was crucial for sustainable growth. He allocated 80% of the budget to essential tools like the website hosting, CRM, and legal databases. The remaining 20% was set aside for exploring and testing new technologies.

This balanced approach allowed Ethan to maintain a robust tech infrastructure while still having the flexibility to innovate—a key factor in staying competitive as a new business. For example, when AI-powered legal research tools began emerging, Ethan had the budget to test and eventually implement one, giving EcoLegal a competitive edge.

"I never thought I'd be excited about AI," Ethan admitted to Olivia. "But seeing how it can enhance our services... it's like having a super-powered legal assistant! This must be how successful tech entrepreneurs feel when they discover a game-changing tool."

Ethan also invested in cybersecurity measures early on, recognizing the importance of protecting sensitive client information. This decision came after a sleepless night following a news story about a law firm that had suffered a data breach.

"Our clients trust us with their information," he told his small team of freelancers. "We have a duty to protect it with everything we've got. This is what will set us apart as a trustworthy new player in the legal tech space."

As EcoLegal continued to grow and evolve, Ethan found himself increasingly comfortable in his role as a tech-savvy entrepreneur. The journey from aspiring entrepreneur to confident business owner hadn't been easy, but by following the S.M.A.R.T. Path to Tech Success, he had transformed both his business idea and himself.

"You know, Olivia," he said one evening, as he shut down his laptop after a productive day, "a year ago, I never would have believed I could do this. Now, I feel like I'm not just running a business, but I'm part of this whole world of legal tech entrepreneurship. It's exciting to think about where EcoLegal might go from here."

Olivia smiled, proud of how far her husband had come. "That's the spirit of a true entrepreneur, Ethan. Always looking ahead to the next challenge."

How S.M.A.R.T. helped Ethan

Ethan Choi's journey from a corporate lawyer to the founder of EcoLegal exemplifies the effective application of the S.M.A.R.T. Path to Tech Success. Let's analyze how each principle played out in his entrepreneurial venture:

He Set Up His Tech Knowledge Early

Ethan recognized the critical importance of building a strong technological foundation from the outset. Despite his initial overwhelm, he committed to a structured learning approach, dedicating specific time each day to different aspects of technology relevant to his business. By utilizing free resources and trials, Ethan gained hands-on experience with essential tools like WordPress, Mailchimp, and HubSpot CRM.

This early investment in knowledge paid off significantly. Within two months, Ethan had developed enough understanding to make informed decisions about EcoLegal's tech infrastructure and communicate effectively with developers. This rapid upskilling was crucial in getting his business off the ground and setting it up for future success.

He Mastered Tech Adaptability

Ethan's willingness to adapt to new technologies was a key factor in EcoLegal's growth. When he noticed the trend towards video content, he pushed past his comfort zone to develop video production skills. This adaptability allowed him to connect with his audience more effectively and differentiate EcoLegal in the market.

By maintaining a "Tech Trends" document, Ethan ensured he stayed informed about emerging technologies relevant to his field. This proactive approach to adaptability positioned EcoLegal to take advantage of new opportunities and stay ahead of competitors.

He Aligned His Tech Stack for Growth

In selecting EcoLegal's tech stack, Ethan demonstrated foresight by prioritizing scalability. His choice of WordPress with WooCommerce for the website and Salesforce for CRM reflected an understanding that his tech infrastructure needed to support long-term growth.

This alignment paid dividends when EcoLegal expanded its services to include personalized legal document preparation. The scalable tech stack allowed for seamless integration of this new offering without requiring a major overhaul, saving time and resources.

He Went Back to Refine His Tech Integration

EcoLegal's efficiency got an enormous boost from Ethan's tech integration. With Zapier, he automated tasks and reduced the chance of making mistakes.

Integrating his legal research database with document preparation software further streamlined his work processes. These efficiencies were crucial for Ethan as a solo entrepreneur, allowing him to manage a growing business without becoming overwhelmed by administrative tasks.

He Budgeted for Sustainable Growth

Ethan's budgeting style showed a good balance between what he needed now and what he wanted in the future. By allocating 80% of his tech budget to essential tools and 20% to exploring new technologies, he ensured EcoLegal had a solid technological foundation while remaining flexible enough to innovate.

This forward-thinking budgeting allowed Ethan to invest in emerging technologies like AI-powered legal research tools, giving EcoLegal a competitive edge. It also enabled him to prioritize cybersecurity measures, building trust with clients and protecting his business from potential data breaches.

Embracing Technology in Your Entrepreneurial Journey

As we've seen through Ethan Choi's journey, technology can be a powerful ally in turning your entrepreneurial vision into reality. But let's be honest, for many of us, the tech world can seem daunting at first. If you're feeling some trepidation about the technical aspects of starting your business, you're not alone. The good news? You've got this, and here's why.

First, let's tackle that tech fear head-on. Remember, you don't need to be a coding wizard or a tech guru to leverage technology effectively in your business. What you do need is curiosity and a willingness to learn. Every tech-savvy entrepreneur started somewhere, and that somewhere is exactly where you are now.

Now, about that learning process – embrace it! Trial and error isn't just okay; it's a crucial part of your journey. Each time you figure out how to use a new tool or solve a tech problem, you're building valuable skills. Think of it as your personal tech boot camp. It might be challenging but the payoff is worth it.

With budgeting for tech, think sustainability. It's not about having the latest gadgets or the most expensive software. It's about choosing the right tools that can grow with your business. Start with what you need now and plan for the future. A thoughtful tech budget can be the difference between a business that thrives and one that struggles to keep up.

Here's something crucial to remember: you are absolutely capable of learning the tech skills your business needs. The human brain is remarkably adaptable, and yours is no exception. With the wealth of resources available today, from online courses to mentorship programs, you have everything you need to become tech-proficient at your fingertips.

Embracing technology as an entrepreneur isn't just about staying current; it's about opening doors to new possibilities. It's about finding innovative ways to bring your unique vision to life. So, take that step forward. Dive into the tech world with confidence. Learn, grow, and watch as technology becomes not just a tool, but a catalyst for your success.

Remember, every tech success story started with someone deciding they could do it. And you know what? You can do it too. Your entrepreneurial adventure is waiting, and it's going to be exciting!

Take a Moment to Reflect

Reflection Questions:

Consider your personal experience as an entrepreneur in the tech industry. Take a moment to think about these questions and be honest with yourself about your current situation and future goals.

- How comfortable are you with your current tech stack? Rate your understanding of the tools you're using and identify areas where you might need to deepen your knowledge.

- What new tech skills have you identified as crucial for your business growth in the next year? Consider both the immediate needs of your business and emerging trends in your industry.

- On a scale of 1 to 10, how would you rate your willingness to learn new technological skills? What factors contribute to this rating, and how might you increase it?

- Looking back over the past twelve months, what new tech skills have you acquired? How have these skills impacted your business, and what are you most proud of learning?

Your responses to these questions can serve as a roadmap for your continued growth in the tech sphere. Remember, embracing technology is an ongoing journey, not a destination.

Action Steps:

Now that you've reflected on your current relationship with technology, it's time to take proactive steps to improve your tech literacy and overcome the challenges outlined in the S.M.A.R.T. Path to Tech Success. These actions help you build confidence, streamline your business, and stay adaptable in a fast-changing tech landscape.

1. Enroll in a Tech Course or Workshop

Choose a course or workshop focused on a specific tech skill you identified as crucial for your business growth. This could learn a new software tool, digital marketing strategies, or data analytics. Set a completion goal and hold yourself accountable by integrating what you've learned into your daily business operations.

PRO TIP: Platforms like Coursera, Udemy, or LinkedIn Learning offer flexible, affordable courses on a wide variety of tech topics. Choose a course that fits your schedule and aligns with your business needs.

2. Audit and Optimize Your Current Tech Stack

Take a deep dive into your current tech stack and evaluate whether your tools are serving your business efficiently. Identify gaps, inefficiencies, or redundancies. Look for ways to automate processes and ensure that all your systems are integrated to improve workflow and save time.

PRO TIP: Schedule a day each quarter to audit your tools. Use software reviews and integration tests to determine whether your current tech stack is scalable and efficient.

3. Experiment with One New Technology

Pick one new tool or platform that you've been curious about or that is emerging in your industry. Start by exploring its free trial or demo version and assess whether it can solve an existing pain point in your business. Don't be afraid to experiment; sometimes, trying out new technology is the only way to learn if it's a good fit.

PRO TIP: Consider tools that offer automation or advanced analytics to help streamline business processes, reduce manual tasks, or provide deeper insights into customer behavior.

4. Build a Tech Support Network

Connect with other entrepreneurs or join online communities where tech knowledge is shared. Surround yourself with people who have a range of tech expertise, whether it's through networking events, mentorship programs, or online forums. This network can be invaluable when you encounter tech challenges, providing guidance and resources to help you navigate the complexities.

PRO TIP: Look for tech-focused entrepreneurial communities on platforms like Reddit, LinkedIn, or industry-specific forums. Building relationships with peers can offer insights and solutions to tech-based challenges that you may not find on your own.

Conclusion: Yes, Tech is for You Too!

Embracing technology as an entrepreneur is not just an option—it's a must in today's digital age. *The S.M.A.R.T. Path to Tech Success* equips you with the knowledge and mindset to confidently navigate this essential part of your business journey. By Setting Up Tech Knowledge, Mastering Adaptability, Aligning Your Tech Stack, Refining Integration, and Tech-Forward Budgeting, you create a solid foundation for business growth. Each of these principles ensures that technology enhances your business operations, making them smoother, more efficient, and scalable.

As you move forward, remember that technology should be a tool that works for you, not an obstacle. Implementing these lessons early in your entrepreneurial journey will ensure that your business can thrive in the digital age, adapt to changes, and maintain long-term success. By following the S.M.A.R.T. Path, you're not just keeping up with technology—you're leveraging it to shape the future of your business.

CHAPTER 10:

Mastering Money Across Borders

"Don't tell me where your priorities are. Show me where you spend your money, and I'll tell you what they are."

–James W. Frick

I don't know if I made the right decision," I confessed, staring at my laptop screen as I spoke to my friend back in the States. "I thought I had enough saved, but it's disappearing so quickly. What if I run out before the business even gets off the ground?"

"You knew this wasn't going to be easy," my friend replied. "But you're resourceful. There's got to be a way to make this work."

Their words stuck with me. I had a huge safety net saved up—years of working long hours and saving diligently had finally paid off. This safety net allowed me to make the leap and fund my living expenses and the setup of ByteBao. But what I quickly learned is that a safety net is just that—a net. It's there to catch you, but it won't last forever.

I remember sitting in my apartment, staring at my laptop as the numbers dwindled. The expenses were piling up faster than I expected—rent, business permits, fees I hadn't accounted for. The safety net that once felt so comforting now seemed to shrink every day. I had thought I could make it stretch for a year, but the reality of starting a business in a new country was different. The costs were higher, and the safety net was depleting at an alarming rate. I felt the weight of the risk I had taken.

I knew I couldn't just sit back and watch my savings disappear. I needed to take action. I started reaching out to my international network, leveraging the connections I had built over the years. It wasn't easy—it meant putting myself out there, asking for help, and being vulnerable about my situation. But it paid off.

A tech company grant supported my educational work in Web3 and blockchain technology. The grant was a lifeline. It allowed me to scale my educational offerings to lawyers, helping them understand blockchain and its implications. This wasn't just about the money—it was about credibility. The grant opened doors to new clients and partnerships that I wouldn't have been able to access otherwise.

I also brought on an advisor who had extensive experience in the tech space. Their insights were invaluable, and they helped me navigate the complexities of setting up a business in Dubai. Through their connections, I was able to secure new partners and clients, slowly but surely building the foundation of ByteBao.

Another lesson I learned was about simplifying my corporate structure. When I first started, I had companies in the US, Singapore, and Dubai. I thought I needed an intricate setup like the one my previous corporate employers had—multiple entities to handle different aspects of the business. But it quickly became overwhelming. The paperwork, the compliance, the sheer number of tax systems I had to deal with—it was too much for one person.

I remember sitting in front of a stack of documents, feeling completely defeated. It felt like every time I made progress, there was another form to fill out, another regulation to comply with. I realized I needed to make a change. I closed the US and Singapore entities and focus solely on Dubai. It was a tough decision—I had put a lot of effort into setting up those companies—but it was the right one. Simplifying my structure made everything more manageable. I could focus on what really mattered: building my business and serving my clients.

There were moments of doubt, moments when I questioned if I had made the right choices. But each challenge taught me something valuable. The safety net was crucial, but it wasn't infinite. The grant and my advisor helped me get back on my feet, and simplifying my structure allowed me to focus my energy where it was needed most.

Looking back, I see the ups and downs as part of the journey. Dubai is now home, and ByteBao is growing in ways I couldn't have imagined. The lesson I want to share is this: have a safety net, but don't rely on it to last forever. Be prepared to pivot, to reach out for support, and to simplify when things get too complicated. Starting a business abroad is challenging, but with the right mindset and strategies, it's also incredibly rewarding.

Rule: Lean on the 4 Pillars of Smart Business Financing Abroad

Successfully managing your finances as an expat entrepreneur can feel overwhelming. Not only are you navigating the complexities of starting a business, but you're also doing it in a foreign country with different financial systems, regulations, and currency risks. The key to thriving in this challenging environment is to take a balanced and practical approach to your business finances. The 4 Pillars of Smart Business Financing Abroad provide a framework that helps you build a sustainable and scalable business while securing your financial future.

1. Set Up a Financial Safety Net

One of the most common mistakes expat entrepreneurs make is starting a new venture without enough personal financial security. Moving abroad comes with uncertainties, differences in cost of living, potential legal hurdles, and unforeseen expenses. Combine this with the risks of starting a business, and the stakes become even higher.

A financial safety net is crucial for managing these unknowns. Whether you face an economic downturn or need emergency funds for unexpected expenses, having a safety net ensures you don't have to rely solely on business income to stay afloat. Aim to save 6–12 months of living expenses before fully committing to your venture. This will give you peace of mind as you navigate the uncertainties of expat life.

PRO TIP: Automate monthly transfers to a high-yield savings account separate from your business accounts. Consider using international banks with low foreign transaction fees and easy access to your funds while living abroad. If you need to send money back home, set up a dedicated fund or use tools like Wise or Remitly to minimize fees and ensure consistency in supporting family obligations. Ensure that your financial safety net includes provisions for healthcare and insurance in your host country.

2. Bootstrap and Generate Early Revenue

A common pitfall is waiting for a perfect, fully developed product before launching. Instead, start small with a Minimum Viable Product (MVP) or a simplified service offering. Bootstrapping—relying on personal savings and early revenue rather than outside investment—allows you to test your business idea, validate market demand, and refine your offerings without over-committing financially.

In the early stages, focus on generating revenue quickly. Offering a reduced version of your product or service allows you to build relationships with early customers and learn from their feedback. This way, you refine your product before scaling.

PRO TIP: Launch a beta version of your product through social media or email marketing. Offer early adopters a discounted price for feedback, which will help you improve your offering.

3. Explore Global and Local Funding Options

Expat entrepreneurs often limit themselves by only considering local funding options. However, as an expat, you have access to global funding sources. Grants, crowdfunding, or even leveraging financial resources from your home country can expand your funding possibilities.

Look into grants from international organizations or industry-specific funding programs. Crowdfunding platforms like Kickstarter and Indiegogo can also connect you with supporters who believe in your vision. Remember, your network is a valuable resource—fellow expats often have connections to investors or grant opportunities that could help you grow.

PRO TIP: Research and apply for at least three grants or funding programs relevant to your industry. Use platforms like Grants.gov or Opengrants.io for international funding opportunities. Consider building local credit by obtaining smaller loans or credit cards to establish a financial presence in your host country.

4. Minimize Financial Risk

Managing financial risk is one of the biggest challenges for expat entrepreneurs. From fluctuating exchange rates to navigating tax laws, risks are inevitable. A proactive approach to financial management can mitigate these challenges.

Ensure you have a solid accounting system that can handle multi-country financial obligations. Hiring a local accountant who understands both your host country and home country tax laws will help you stay compliant and avoid costly mistakes. Currency fluctuations can also be a risk—using multi-currency accounts or hedging strategies can protect your profits. Be mindful of tax residency and double taxation treaties that may affect your liabilities in both countries.

PRO TIP: Hire a bilingual accountant, if needed, to help you manage tax compliance in both countries. Use tools like Wise or Revolut for cross-border transactions to minimize fees and currency risks. Consider using multi-currency accounts to reduce conversion fees, and research hedging options like forward contracts to manage exchange rate risk. Make life easier by setting up automatic transfers for your responsibilities back home, so you can focus on your personal and family commitments.

Bringing It All Together: Jenna's Story

Jenna sat at her favorite coffee shop in Toronto, nursing her iced latte while listening to her friends' concerns. She was 32, single, with no kids, and tired of her corporate life in Canada. The idea of moving to Bali to start a wellness retreat had taken root in her mind, but her friends were not on board.

"Jenna, this is crazy," her friend Michelle said, shaking her head. "Do you know how financially risky this is? You don't even have a steady income lined up over there. What if it doesn't work out?"

"I know it's risky, but I've thought it through," Jenna insisted, her voice more confident than she felt. "I've been saving for years, and I've got enough to support myself for at least ten months. Besides, I can't keep living this life. I'm burned out. I need a change."

Her other friend, Lisa, chimed in, "But what if you run out of money before your business even takes off? Bali isn't Canada. You're dealing with a different currency, a different culture. It's not going to be easy."

Jenna took a deep breath. She appreciated her friends' concern, but she knew deep down that she couldn't let fear dictate her life any longer. Years of late nights at a company that didn't care about her well-being left her feeling trapped. She wanted meaningful work.

"I've got to try," she said finally, her eyes meeting theirs. "Even if it doesn't work out, at least I'll know I gave it my best shot. I need to do this for myself."

A few weeks later, Jenna stepped off a plane into the humid warmth of Bali. The air was thick with the scent of incense and tropical flowers, and the distant sound of scooters buzzed in the background. She felt a mix of exhilaration and anxiety as she made her way to her temporary villa. This was it—the beginning of her new chapter.

But the reality of setting up a business in a foreign country soon set in. On her second day in Bali, Jenna visited a local market to buy some essentials. As she handed over a crisp 100,000 rupiah note, she realized she did not know if she was overpaying. The numbers felt overwhelming, and she struggled to convert the costs in her head.

"Why does everything have so many zeros?" she muttered to herself, frustrated. It was exhausting, trying to make sense of a new currency while figuring out the cost of everyday items. She found herself second-guessing every purchase, worried she was being taken advantage of simply because she didn't understand.

Jenna had initially planned to rent a small space for her yoga classes, but she quickly realized that rental prices were higher than expected in the popular areas of Bali. Her savings were dwindling faster than she had expected, and the stress of not knowing whether her business would take off weighed heavily on her.

One night, after another frustrating day of trying to navigate the complexities of permits and pricing, Jenna video-called Michelle. Tears brimmed in her eyes as she confessed, "I don't know if I can do this. Everything is so much harder than I thought. The currency, the paperwork, the costs—it's all so overwhelming."

"Jenna, you knew this wasn't going to be easy," Michelle said gently. "But you're one of the most determined people I know. You just need a plan."

Michelle's words stuck with Jenna. That night, she took a step back and reassess. She remembered reading about a framework called the "4 Pillars of Smart Business Financing" for expat entrepreneurs. She put it into action.

The first step was setting up a financial safety net. Jenna realized she needed to stabilize her finances before pushing forward with the retreat. She reached out to her network back in Canada and picked up a few freelance wellness coaching clients. The income from these clients helped her cover her living expenses without dipping further into her savings.

Next, Jenna embraced the idea of bootstrapping. Instead of renting an expensive studio space, she started small by offering private yoga and mindfulness sessions at local hotels and guesthouses. She created a simple three-module mindfulness workshop that she could deliver anywhere—on a beach, in a garden, or even at someone's villa. This allowed her to generate early revenue without being over-committed financially.

Jenna also researched grants for wellness initiatives and found an international wellness foundation that offered small grants for women entrepreneurs. After a detailed application, she was thrilled to receive $5,000 in funding, which she used to expand her marketing efforts and purchase better equipment for her workshops.

Managing financial risk became her next focus. Jenna hired a local accountant who spoke both English and Bahasa Indonesia, someone who understood the tax regulations in both Canada and Indonesia. The accountant helped her set up a multi-currency account, making it easier to manage her earnings from both her Canadian clients and her local workshops. She also started using Wise for cross-border transactions, which saved her money on conversion fees.

Slowly, things fell into place. Jenna felt a sense of relief as she saw her savings stabilize and her business growing. She had a small but loyal group of clients who loved her mindfulness workshops, and she was building connections within the local wellness community. The anxiety that had gripped her in those early weeks faded, replaced by a sense of purpose and determination.

One evening, as she watched the sun set over the ocean, Jenna felt a wave of calm wash over her. She had done it. She had faced her fears, tackled the obstacles, and was finally seeing her dream come to life. Bali was no longer just an escape—it was home, and her wellness retreat was thriving.

Jenna called Michelle that night. "You were right," she said, her voice filled with emotion. "It wasn't easy. But I'm so glad I didn't give up. I feel like I'm finally living the life I was meant to live."

"I knew you could do it," Michelle replied, her smile evident even through the phone. "You just needed to trust yourself."

Jenna hung up, a smile on her face. She had trusted herself, and it had made all the difference.

Take a Moment to Reflect

It's time to dive into a practical reflection—one that will help you map out your finances and create a strategy to manage your safety net, funding sources, and expenses. Use the following worksheet to guide your planning and ensure you're prepared for the challenges of starting a business abroad.

Doing the Work: Financial Planning for your Venture Abroad

1. Identify Your Safety Net

- *How much do you have saved?*

- Total amount saved: _____

- How many months of living expenses will this cover? _____

- Are there any additional emergency funds you can access if needed? _____

2. Projected Expenses

- *List all of your projected expenses for the first year.*

- Living expenses (rent, utilities, groceries, etc.): _____

- Business setup costs (permits, licenses, equipment): _____

- Marketing and client acquisition: _____

- Miscellaneous (unexpected fees, health expenses, etc.): _____

3. Income Sources

- *What are your current or potential income sources?*

- Existing clients or freelance work: _____

- Grants or funding options: _____

- Revenue from product/service sales: _____

- Other potential sources (e.g., investments, part-time work): _____

4. Funding Strategy

- *How can you secure additional funding if needed?*

- List three potential grants or funding programs you can apply for: _____

- Are there crowdfunding options you could explore? _____

- Could you leverage your network for financial support or partnerships? _____

5. Expense Management

- *How will you manage your finances to minimize risk?*

- Do you have an accountant or financial advisor who understands both local and international tax laws? _____

- Are you using multi-currency accounts to minimize conversion fees? _____

- What tools will you use to track your expenses and revenue? _____

6. Timeline

- *Create a timeline for your financial goals.*
- Month 1–3: Establish basic income streams to cover initial expenses.
- Month 4–6: Apply for grants, expand client base, and stabilize revenue.
- Month 7–12: Assess the sustainability of your safety net, adjust expenses, and explore new funding opportunities.

Conclusion

Starting a business in a new country is never easy, but it is possible with the right preparation and mindset. My journey in Dubai taught me the importance of having a safety net, but also the need to adapt, simplify, and seek support when needed. Similarly, Jenna faced her own challenges in Bali, navigating the financial and cultural complexities of starting her wellness retreat. Both of our stories are reminders that while the road may be uncertain and full of obstacles, it is not impossible if you put in the work.

Reflect on your own situation. Use the workbook to outline your safety net, your funding sources, and your expenses. Embrace the reality that challenges will arise, but know that with perseverance and a strategic approach, you can build the business and life you dream of. The journey may be tough, but the rewards are worth every step.

CHAPTER 11

Visa Hacks for Entrepreneurs

"Obstacles are those frightful things you see when you take your eyes off your goal."

–Henry Ford

When I first got to Dubai in December 2021, the weather was perfect—sunny with a gentle breeze. I remember stepping out of the airport, my eyes widening at the sight of towering skyscrapers gleaming under the sun, and feeling an exhilarating blend of excitement and uncertainty. I was here to start a new chapter, not just for myself, but for my entire family. And I had made it possible through a creative use of Dubai's remote work visa program.

Earlier that year, I had established my company in Singapore. It was a small but thriving business, providing consulting services that allowed me to work with clients from around the world. The flexibility of my work meant I could essentially work from anywhere, and that's when I started dreaming about relocating. I wanted something different for my family—a new adventure, a lifestyle that would allow us to grow and experience a new culture together. Dubai had always fascinated me with its blend of modernity, tradition, and endless opportunities. It seemed like the perfect place to make that dream a reality.

I remember sitting at the dining table one night, scrolling through my laptop, when my husband looked over at me, a puzzled expression on his face.

"How are we going to move there if we don't have jobs yet?" he asked, his brow furrowed.

I smiled, excited to share what I had discovered. "That's the thing," I said, turning the screen towards him. "Dubai has this new remote work visa program. It's perfect for us. I can leverage the Singapore company I set up and apply as an employee. It meets all the income requirements. We don't need a job here to move—we just need this visa."

He leaned closer, scanning the information on the screen. "Really? It's that simple?"

"It really is," I nodded. "The process is pretty straightforward—there's paperwork, of course, and we'll need to show proof of income, but it's all doable. Once it's approved, we get residency permits, Emirates IDs, everything. It's like we're actual residents here, with access to everything—housing, banking, schools. And I can sponsor you and the kids until we're all set."

He looked at me, a mix of hope and caution in his eyes. "Are you sure it's going to work?"

"Trust me," I said, squeezing his hand. "I've done my research. And when we went in for our medicals, everything was super smooth. We got checked in, did our tests, and it all went faster than I expected. They've really streamlined the process."

He exhaled, a smile slowly spreading across his face. "Okay. Let's do it."

When my visa was finally approved, I felt an overwhelming sense of relief and accomplishment. It wasn't just a piece of paper—it was the key to a new beginning. With my newly granted visa, I received a residency permit, which meant I could now get my Emirates ID, something that was essential to truly feeling like I belonged. The Emirates ID opened up access to everything other residents had—from setting up bank accounts to getting a local SIM card, renting a home, and even registering my kids for school.

One of the most rewarding aspects of this experience was being able to sponsor my husband and children. It meant that we could all move together, and that I was the one paving the way for our family's new adventure. I remember the day we all stepped into our new apartment. The kids ran around exploring every corner, their laughter echoing off the empty walls. My husband and I exchanged a look that said it all—we had done it. We had uprooted our lives and create something entirely new, in a place that was brimming with possibilities.

Settling in wasn't without its challenges. There were days when the bureaucracy felt overwhelming—the appointments, the forms, the waiting. There were moments when I wondered if we had made the right choice. But then there were also mornings spent watching the sun rise over the desert, family picnics at the beach, and evenings exploring the bustling souks that seemed to make it all worthwhile. I learned to navigate the systems, and over time, things became easier. The initial challenges gave way to a sense of belonging.

I share this story because I know how daunting it can feel to think about moving to a new country, especially with a family in tow. The logistics can feel overwhelming, and the idea of leaving behind the familiar for the unknown can be terrifying. But the truth is, today there are so many programs designed to help people like us—people who want to work remotely, who want to build businesses, who want to experience life in a new place. The remote work visa made it possible for me to bring my business and my family to Dubai, to take that leap without the fear of being stuck in visa limbo or dealing with impossible requirements.

If you have an existing business, or if you work remotely, there are opportunities out there for you. The key is to do your research and be prepared to put in the effort. The process might seem complex at first, but once you're standing in your new home, watching your children adapt to their new surroundings, you'll know it was all worth it. For us, Dubai has become a place of growth, both personally and professionally. The city's energy is infectious, and being surrounded by so many ambitious people has motivated me to dream even bigger for my business.

Using the remote work visa to come to Dubai allowed me to craft a life that feels aligned with what I value—freedom, family, and opportunity. It gave me the chance to immerse myself in a new culture, provide new experiences for my children, and continue growing my business on my own terms. The experience taught me that sometimes, all it takes is a bit of creativity and courage to change your life completely. If you're considering making a move, don't let the fear of logistics hold you back. The opportunities are out there, and they're more accessible than ever.

Dubai welcomed us with open arms, and it could do the same for you. Whether it's through a remote work visa, an entrepreneur permit, or another program, the path to building a life abroad is there—you just have to take the first step.

And now that you've seen how it worked for me, let's dive into how you can use these visa programs to design your freedom and create a life that aligns with your dreams.

Rule: Use Visa Programs to Design Your Freedom

In today's connected world, building your dream business or working remotely from another country is more doable than ever. One great way to make this happen is by taking advantage of the many visa programs available for remote workers, entrepreneurs, and digital nomads. By using these programs, you can create a lifestyle that fits you, while building a business that aligns with your goals.

Countries around the world recognize the value that remote workers, freelancers, and entrepreneurs bring to their economies, and they've made it easier for you to settle in through specialized visa programs. As an expat, you have a lot of options—from remote work visas to entrepreneur permits—all designed to make your move to a new country smoother and more accessible.

Step 1: Explore Your Visa Options

The rise of remote work has shifted how governments think about immigration. Many countries that used to restrict work visas to traditional corporate jobs are now welcoming remote workers to come experience their culture and contribute to their economy. These visas, often called "digital nomad visas," allow you to live in a country while working remotely, whether you're with a company or freelancing. Imagine working on your business while enjoying the beaches of Barbados, the vibrant cities of Portugal, or the cultural richness of Croatia.

If you're interested in setting up a more permanent business presence, there are also entrepreneur visas available. Countries like Singapore, the United Arab Emirates, and Chile offer programs specifically for entrepreneurs. These visas often require a business plan, proof of funding, and a commitment to invest in the local economy, making them perfect for those who are ready to take their business to the next level.

Step 2: Inventory Your Financial Situation

Before diving into visa opportunities, it's important to inspect your financial resources. Each visa program comes with its own requirements. Some remote work visas need you to show proof of a stable income, while entrepreneur visas might ask for proof of investment capital or a financial safety net to cover your living expenses while you get started.

Understanding your finances will help you figure out which visa option is best for you. If you're self-funded and want more flexibility, a digital nomad visa could be a great fit. These visas usually have fewer requirements and let you work from wherever suits you. If you have significant capital and a specific business idea you want to bring to life, an entrepreneur visa could give you the support and stability you need to make it happen.

Step 3: Overcome Visa Anxiety

In the past, the idea of moving abroad was often intimidating because of complicated visa requirements and the fear of rejection. But things are changing fast. Governments are increasingly aware of the benefits that remote workers and entrepreneurs bring to their countries, and they are creating more accessible programs to attract people like you. So, there's no need to feel anxious about the visa process anymore.

There are now plenty of straightforward options available. The key is to do your research, match a visa program to your financial situation and business goals, and take the leap. Whether you want to work remotely while experiencing a new culture or set up a thriving business in a new market, there's a visa out there that can help you make it happen.

Step 4: Design the Life You Want

These visa programs give you the freedom to create the life you want. Are you dreaming of working from a beachside villa, or growing your business in a bustling city? Maybe you want to spend a few years in one country and then move on to the next adventure.

The options are out there to help you create a lifestyle that brings you joy, freedom, and fulfillment. By choosing the right visa program, you can make the move to a new country much easier and turn your vision for your life and business into reality. The perfect visa for your dream life is waiting to help you get there.

Now that we've explored how visa programs can help you design your ideal life, let's look at how one entrepreneur made the leap. Meet Peter, an Irish business owner who took advantage of Dubai's investor partner visa to start his wellness venture.

CASE STUDY: PETER'S WELLNESS DREAM TAKES ROOT

Peter stood at the departure gate, taking a deep breath as he looked back at the bustling airport. The noise of announcements, people chatting, and suitcases rolling across the floor filled the air, but his mind was on what awaited him in Dubai. This was it. He was taking the leap, moving to Dubai to start a new chapter not only for himself but also for his family. His wife, Aoife, and their two children were back in Ireland, waiting for him to get everything set up before joining him. It was a decision they had made together—they didn't want to uproot the kids from school until they were sure everything was settled.

Peter had spent years running his gym business in Ireland. He had built something he was proud of, but he couldn't shake the feeling that there was more out there for him. Dubai had caught his attention for a long time—it seemed vibrant, full of life, and, more importantly, a market that was mushrooming in the wellness sector. He knew that his concept for a high-end gym focused on busy professionals would be a perfect fit. The opportunity was too good to pass up.

He had some existing customers who were excited about the idea of an international expansion, and with enough money saved up, he took advantage of Dubai's investor partner visa. The process was relatively straightforward, but Peter had decided to hire someone locally to help with the setup. He knew the value of time, and with his family relying on him, he wanted everything to be as smooth as possible. Sitting in his office in Dublin, he'd made the arrangements. He had hired a consultant in Dubai who knew the ins and outs of the local bureaucracy and could set up his business on his behalf.

Now, here he was, stepping off the plane into the desert heat, ready to get things going. As soon as he arrived, Peter went straight to complete the paperwork. The consultant he'd hired had already laid the groundwork. All Peter needed to do was sign a few forms, take his medical exam, and finish the Emirates ID process. It was surprisingly efficient. He remembered texting Aoife after the medical exam, telling her how quickly it all went.

"Everything's going great here," he typed. "Medical done, and just waiting for the Emirates ID now. Should be sorted in a week."

Aoife's reply came quickly: "That's amazing! The kids will be so excited to hear that everything is moving fast."

Peter smiled, feeling a rush of relief. He could picture his kids' faces lighting up at the thought of joining him soon. It was tough being apart, but knowing they'd be back soon made the sacrifice worth it. He had promised Aoife that he wouldn't bring them over until he was sure that everything—the apartment, the bank accounts, the school registrations—was sorted. He wanted their transition to be seamless.

The following days were a whirlwind. Peter navigated Dubai's bustling streets, taking in the towering skyscrapers and the endless construction that seemed to signal a city in constant growth. He spent his mornings finishing the paperwork and his afternoons exploring potential locations for his gym. He had his eyes on a spot near the financial district, a place where busy professionals could easily access after work or during a lunch break. He could already envision the space—sleek, modern, with all the latest equipment and amenities to cater to Dubai's ambitious crowd.

One evening, as he sat on the balcony of his temporary apartment, watching the sun dip below the horizon, Peter felt a sense of calm wash over him. It had been a hectic week, but everything was falling into place. He had already opened a local bank account, a task he thought would be daunting, but turned out to be straightforward with his investor visa. He had even started making connections in the local wellness community, reaching out to other entrepreneurs and getting a feel for the market. The excitement of building something new, in a place so full of possibilities, was invigorating.

He called Aoife that night. She answered almost immediately; her face appearing on the screen, framed by the familiar background of their living room in Ireland.

"Hey, love! How's everything?" she asked, her eyes bright with curiosity.

"It's going really well," Peter said, leaning back in his chair. "I've got the bank account set up, finished with the Emirates ID application today. I even found a few potential spots for the gym."

"That's incredible, Peter," Aoife said, her voice filled with pride. "I knew you'd make it work. The kids are counting down the days until we can come over."

"I can't wait to have you all here," Peter said, his voice softening. "I think you'll love it. The city's got this energy—like anything is possible. And I really believe the gym is going to be a hit. There's such a demand here for wellness, especially for guys like me—busy professionals who need a place to unwind and stay fit."

Aoife smiled. "I believe in you. And I know the kids will love the adventure. Just make sure you're taking care of yourself, too."

Peter chuckled. "I am. Don't worry. I'm even getting my own workouts in—testing out the competition," he added with a wink.

By the end of the week, Peter had his Emirates ID in hand. It felt almost surreal—just days ago, he had been in Ireland, and now here he was, a resident of Dubai, with everything set up to start his new venture. He had opened the bank accounts, secured a location for his gym, and even started making friends. The next step was bringing Aoife and the kids over, and he couldn't wait to show them the life he was building for all of them.

Peter knew the journey was just beginning. There would be challenges ahead—setting up the gym, attracting clients, navigating a new culture—but he was ready for it. Dubai had already shown him it was a city where dreams could become reality if you will put in the effort. And Peter was ready to do just that. This move wasn't just about business—it was about giving his family a fresh experience, a new adventure, and a chance to grow together in a place that was full of promise.

Peter's story is a perfect example of how using the right visa program can simplify moving abroad and setting up a business. But what about you? Let's reflect on how you can apply these strategies to your own situation and create the life you envision.

Take a Moment to Reflect

Peter's journey shows that taking the leap into a new country is often more straightforward than we think—especially if we take advantage of the right visa opportunities. Whether you're thinking of moving as an entrepreneur or working remotely, the key is to align your actions with your vision of the life you want. Let's reflect on how you can apply these ideas to your own circumstances.

First, it's essential to determine whether you want to move as an entrepreneur or as a remote worker. Each option comes with its own benefits and challenges, and understanding where you fit can help you take the next steps confidently.

- **Entrepreneur Visa**: Are you someone who wants to start a business abroad or expand an existing one? If so, an entrepreneur visa could be the perfect fit for you. This path is great if you have a clear business idea, some existing customers, and enough capital to invest in a new market. Think about what kind of business you want to create. What industry excites you? What country would be the best fit for your business? Countries like Dubai, Singapore, and Chile offer entrepreneur visas that could give you the opportunity to build something meaningful while immersing yourself in a new culture.

- **Remote Work Visa**: On the other hand, if you're employed by a company or work freelance, you might consider a remote work visa. These visas allow you to work from anywhere while enjoying the experience of living in a new country. Ask yourself: Where do you want to live? Do you enjoy the freedom of working from different locations? Countries like Portugal, Croatia, and Barbados offer digital nomad visas that make it easier for remote workers to live and work there.

Taking Inventory of Your Situation

Once you know whether you want to move as an entrepreneur or a remote worker, it's time to take stock of your current situation.

- **Finances**: Do you have enough capital to invest in starting a business abroad? What are your sources of income, and how steady are they? Consider what visa options best align with your financial situation. Entrepreneur visas might require you to show proof of investment capital, while remote work visas often have an income requirement.

- **Research Visa Options**: Research the countries that offer visas aligned with your goals. Understand the requirements and processes involved. Are there countries that particularly attract you? Each country has different regulations, so identifying what best fits your situation is a crucial step.

- **Define Your Why**: Why do you want to move? Is it to experience a new culture, to grow your business, or to enjoy a change in lifestyle? Your "why" will help keep you motivated throughout the visa process and the initial challenges of moving.

Reflection Questions:

To help you apply these ideas to your own life, consider journaling on the following prompts:

- What does your ideal day look like in a new country? Are you running your own business or working remotely?

- What excites you about relocating? What are you hoping to gain from the experience?

- What is one action you can take today to move towards making this dream a reality?

By reflecting on these questions, you can chart your path towards living and working abroad, using the same strategies that made Peter's journey possible.

Take Action:

Reflecting on your situation is important, but taking action is what will turn your dream into reality. Here are some practical steps to get started:

- **Identify Your Ideal Location**: Choose the country that aligns best with your personal and professional goals.

- **Gather Your Documents**: Start compiling the paperwork for the visa. This might include proof of income, business plans, bank statements, or employment contracts.

- **Connect with Local Experts**: If you can, hire a consultant or reach out to local experts who understand the visa process in the country you're considering. Their expertise can save you a lot of time and hassle.

Conclusion

As we close this chapter, take a moment to envision the life you want to create. Visa programs are not just bureaucratic tools—they're gateways to designing a life that aligns with your goals and values. Whether it's running your dream business in a thriving market or working remotely from a picturesque location, the possibilities are endless when you take that first step. Peter's story is a testament to what's possible when you combine preparation with bold action. Now, it's your turn to reflect on how these strategies can work for you. What excites you about this journey? What steps can you take today to move closer to your vision of freedom and fulfillment?

Remember, the hardest part is often just starting. By taking small, intentional steps, you'll be well on your way to creating a life that blends adventure, opportunity, and purpose. The world is waiting for you—so why not take the leap?

PART IV

Living Your Vision

CHAPTER 12

Build a Business that Works for You

"Success isn't about how much money you make; it's about the difference you make in people's lives."

–Michelle Obama

The cool air of the conference center was a welcome relief as I shrugged off my blazer, still buzzing from moderating panels and group discussions at the Digital Assets Asia 2024 conference. It was April 2024, and the symposium in Hong Kong was in full swing. As I scanned the crowd, a familiar face caught my eye.

"Claire!" I called out, waving to the lawyer I'd known virtually for months but was meeting in person for the first time. She made her way through the crowd, a warm smile on her face.

"That was an incredible presentation," Claire said as we hugged. "Your insights on regulatory challenges were spot on."

I felt a surge of pride and excitement. "Thanks, Claire. It's so great to finally meet you in person. How about we grab a coffee and chat?"

As we walked to a nearby table, we reminisced about our expat origin stories comparing timelines of when we were living in Asia and what we were doing at various points in time.

Over steaming cups of coffee, Claire and I dove into a passionate discussion about the future of digital assets in fashion and media. "You know," I said, stirring my coffee thoughtfully, "I'm actually interviewing Vogue Singapore tomorrow about their use of Web3 and NFTs. It's fascinating how they're incorporating this technology into their business model."

Claire's eyes lit up. "That sounds incredible. Will this be for your podcast, *Barely Legal in Web3*?"

I nodded, feeling a familiar excitement building. "Yes, we're recording at a studio in Singapore. I'll be flying out tomorrow. It's part of a series I'm doing on innovative uses of blockchain technology across different industries."

As we continued our conversation, I couldn't help but reflect on how far I'd come in the two years since starting ByteBao. From the uncertainty of leaving my corporate job to now, sitting in Singapore, discussing cutting-edge technology with brilliant minds, it was a journey I couldn't have imagined.

The next morning, I found myself in a sleek recording studio, adjusting my microphone as I prepared to interview the team from Vogue Singapore. The studio hummed with energy, and I felt that familiar flow state wash over me as we began our conversation.

"So, tell me," I began, leaning in with genuine curiosity, "how did Vogue Singapore first decide to explore Web3 and NFTs in your design and business model?"

As the publisher of Vogue Singapore shared her journey of merging high fashion with blockchain technology, I found myself fascinated by the intersection of creativity and innovation. We discussed the challenges of introducing digital art to a traditional fashion audience, the potential of NFTs to revolutionize ownership in the fashion world, and the technical hurdles they'd overcome.

"One of our biggest challenges," she shared, "was explaining the value of digital fashion to our readers. But once they saw the possibilities–exclusive digital couture, blockchain-verified authenticity–they were hooked."

I nodded, thinking of my own journey explaining complex tech concepts to my audience. "It's amazing how technology can open up new realms of creativity and engagement. Have you found that this digital shift has changed your relationship with your audience?"

The conversation flowed effortlessly, and before I knew it, our scheduled hour had flown by. As we wrapped up the recording, I felt a deep sense of fulfillment. This exchange of ideas, this exploration of how technology was shaping diverse industries, this was what I did.

After the interview, I stepped out onto the busy Singapore street, the humidity enveloping me like a warm blanket. I pulled out my phone and dialed home, eager to share the day's experiences with my family.

"Mommy!" my daughter's voice chirped through the speaker. "Did you see any mermaids?"

I laughed, her innocent question grounding me in the simple joys of motherhood. "No mermaids today, sweetheart, but I did see some amazing digital fashion art. It's like magic on a computer!"

"Can you show me when you come home?"

"Absolutely, and guess what? I'm bringing home some of that yummy pineapple cake you liked last time."

Her squeal of delight warmed my heart. As I chatted with my husband and kids, sharing snippets of my day and hearing about theirs, I felt a profound sense of gratitude. ByteBao had given me this–the ability to pursue my passions while staying connected to what mattered most.

That evening, as I stood on the balcony of my hotel room, the Singapore skyline glittered before me, a testament to human innovation and ambition. A gentle breeze carried the faint scent of frangipani, and in the distance, I could hear the soft lapping of waves against the shore.

I closed my eyes, letting the sensations wash over me. Two years ago, when I left my corporate job to start ByteBao, I had been full of uncertainty. I knew I wanted to combine my love for law, technology, and global business, but the path forward had been hazy at best.

Now, standing here in Singapore, having just participated in a regional conference and recorded a fascinating podcast episode, I felt a clarity I'd never experienced before. ByteBao had evolved into more than just a business, it was a means to continually learn, create, and connect.

As I turned in for the night, my mind drifted to the next day's agenda. I had one more podcast recording scheduled, a meeting with a potential ByteBao partner, and then–the part I was looking forward to most–an afternoon off to take my kids (who were flying in with my husband in the morning) to the Singapore Zoo.

This was the life I had dreamed of–a perfect blend of intellectual stimulation, creative expression, global exploration, and quality family time. ByteBao hadn't just become a successful business; it had become the vehicle for a life lived on my own terms.

As sleep overtook me, I felt a deep sense of contentment. The path hadn't always been easy, but it had been unquestionably worth it. In pursuing a life-driven business, I had found more than success, I had found myself.

Rule: Build a Life-Driven Business

A life-driven business is a revolutionary approach to entrepreneurship that seamlessly integrates your skills, passions, and experiences while aligning with the lifestyle you aspire to live. This concept goes beyond traditional business models, encouraging you to build an enterprise that extends who you are, rather than molding yourself to fit into predefined industry structures.

For expat entrepreneurs, this approach is powerful. Your journey across borders and adaptation to new environments has equipped you with a unique blend of skills and perspectives. A life-driven business leverages this diversity, turning it into a competitive advantage. It allows you to design a business that not only reflects your personal journey and global experiences but also enhances, rather than competes with, your personal life.

Key Principles of a Life—Driven Business

- **Self-Awareness**: Understanding and appreciating the unique blend of skills, passions, and experiences you bring to the table is crucial. This self-knowledge forms the foundation of your life-driven business.

- **Strategic Synergy**: Discover how different parts of your life—professional, personal, and cultural—can complement one another to create something truly distinctive. This synergy is where innovation often happens.

- **Lifestyle Alignment**: Your business should support the way you want to live. Whether that means location independence, flexible hours, or the ability to pursue personal passions alongside your work, your business should be a vehicle for achieving your ideal lifestyle.

- **Value Creation**: Leverage your unique perspective to create value in ways that others might not see. Use your cross-cultural experiences and personal insights to offer innovative solutions to market problems.

- **Adaptability**: Allow your business to grow and evolve as you do. Your entrepreneurial path should be fluid, adapting to new opportunities, skills, and market needs as they arise.

Practical Steps to Building a Life-Driven Business

Creating a life-driven business isn't just a lofty concept—it's a practical, actionable framework. By following these steps, you can build a business that not only stands out in the market but also enhances your quality of life.

1. Personal Inventory & Skills Mapping

Begin by taking a comprehensive stock of your entire skill set, experiences, and passions. Write everything, even skills or hobbies that don't seem immediately related to business. Often, unexpected synergies arise when you examine the full picture of what you bring to the table.

2. Craft Your Business Around Your Ideal Life

Envision what your ideal day would look like, both personally and professionally. How many hours do you work? Where are you located? What kind of work are you doing? Use this vision as a framework to shape your business model, ensuring that it aligns with the lifestyle you want to create.

3. Leverage Cross-Cultural Insights

As an expat, your global experiences can serve as a powerful differentiator. Use the unique insights you've gained from living in different cultures to identify market gaps, offer solutions, or target under-served audiences.

4. Start Small, Think Big

Begin by testing your business idea with minimal offerings that tap into at least two of your skill sets. This approach allows you to validate your concept without over committing resources.

5. Storytelling as a Branding Tool

Your journey—whether it's about moving abroad, adapting to new cultures, or pivoting in your career—is a powerful tool for marketing. Craft a compelling narrative about how your life experiences uniquely qualify you to solve certain problems or meet specific market needs.

PRO TIP: Develop a short "origin story" for your business that highlights your unique journey. Use this in your marketing materials, pitches, and networking events to create a memorable brand identity.

6. Set Lifestyle-Aligned Goals

Your business goals should reflect more than just financial targets. Set objectives around flexibility, work-life balance, and personal fulfillment to ensure that your business supports the lifestyle you desire.

Living the Life-Driven Business Philosophy

A life-driven business is about more than just profits or scaling—it's about creating something that feels authentic to you and aligns with your entire self. By integrating your skills, experiences, and passions, and ensuring your business supports your desired lifestyle, you'll craft a fulfilling entrepreneurial journey that reflects who you truly are.

Remember, this approach doesn't mean your business will be easy or free from challenges. However, when obstacles arise, you'll find yourself more resilient and motivated to overcome them because your business is intrinsically tied to your personal growth and life goals.

As you build your life-driven business, stay flexible and open to evolution. Your passions, skills, and life goals may change over time, and your business should be able to adapt accordingly. Regular reflection and willingness to pivot are key to maintaining alignment between your business and your life.

CASE STUDY: FARAH'S PATH TO A LIFE-DRIVEN LIVELIHOOD

The rhythmic tapping of Farrah's fingers on her keyboard echoed through her Dubai apartment as she finished another project plan. The clock on her desk read 11:30 PM, and a deep sigh escaped her lips. She glanced at the framed photo of her daughter and felt a pang of guilt. Another late night at work meant another bedtime story missed.

As she shut down her computer, her eyes landed on a colorful sculpture made of bottle caps and recycled plastic sitting on her bookshelf–a creation from one of her daughter's school projects. A small smile played on her lips as she remembered helping her with it, the joy of creating something beautiful from discarded materials.

The next evening, as Farrah helped her daughter with another art project, this time about environmental conservation, her daughter's innocent question struck a chord. "Mama, why don't you make art that helps the planet?"

Farrah's hand, holding a paintbrush, froze in midair. The question echoed in her mind, stirring something deep within her. "I... I don't know, sweetheart," she replied, her voice barely a whisper.

That night, sleep eluded Farrah. Her mind raced with possibilities. She had always been passionate about sustainability and art, but her career in project management had taken her down a different path. As she tossed and turned, fragments of ideas took shape.

The next morning, fueled by determination and countless cups of Arabic coffee, Farrah began to map out her skills and passions. Her project management expertise, her understanding of the tech industry, her artistic abilities, her love for the environment, and her deep connection to Middle Eastern culture, all these elements swirled in her mind, gradually coalescing into a vision.

Weeks passed, filled with late-night planning sessions and weekend experiments with sustainable materials. The dining table became a makeshift art studio, much to her daughter's delight. "Mama, can I help?" became a frequent question, and Farrah bonded with her daughter in a way she had never had before.

One sunny afternoon, as they worked together on a sculpture made from reclaimed wood and recycled metal, Farrah shared her dream with her daughter. "What if Mama started a company that makes beautiful art to help the environment? And teaches others to do the same?"

Her daughter's eyes widened with excitement. "Can we call it EcoArt, Mama? Like eco-friendly art?"

Farrah laughed, hugging her daughter close. "That's perfect, habibti. EcoArt MENA it is!"

The journey wasn't easy. Farrah's first attempts to secure clients were met with skepticism. "Sustainable art? In office spaces?" one potential client scoffed. But Farrah persisted, drawing on her project management skills to organize her time and resources efficiently.

Her breakthrough came when a former colleague from her tech days visited her small home studio. The air was thick with the scent of eco-friendly paints and reclaimed wood as Farrah unveiled her latest creation, a stunning wall installation made entirely of recycled materials, intricately designed with traditional Arabic patterns.

"This... this is incredible, Farrah," her colleague breathed, running her fingers over the textured surface. "Our new office lobby needs something exactly like this. Can you do it?"

From that first commission, word spread quickly. Farrah's unique blend of environmental consciousness, artistic skill, and understanding of corporate needs struck a chord in the Dubai business community.

As EcoArt MENA grew, Farrah was careful to structure her business around her life with Amira. She set up a studio close to Amira's school, scheduling client meetings and workshops during school hours. Evenings were sacred—time for family, for storytelling, for dreaming up new ideas together.

Two years flew by, and EcoArt MENA expanded beyond Dubai. Farrah found herself in boardrooms in Abu Dhabi, Riyadh, and Doha, presenting her vision for large-scale sustainable art installations. But it was the educational workshops that truly set her soul on fire.

Standing before a group of wide-eyed students in a Doha classroom, Farrah felt a surge of purpose as she taught them to create art from recycled materials. "Every piece of trash has potential," she told them, her voice passionate. "Just like every one of you has the potential to make a difference."

As she walked out of the classroom that day, the hot Gulf sun beating down on her, Farrah felt a profound sense of contentment. She had created more than just a business, she had built a life that aligned with her values, allowed her to express her creativity, and gave her the flexibility to be there for her daughter.

That evening, as Farrah and her daughter sat on their balcony, watching the Dubai skyline shimmer in the twilight, her daughter asked, "Mama, are you happy now?"

Farrah pulled her daughter close, breathing in the sweet scent of her hair mingled with the salt in the air. "Yes, habibti," she replied, her voice thick with emotion. "Mama is very happy. We're making beautiful things and helping the planet, all while spending time together. This is the life I always dreamed of."

As the first stars appeared in the darkening sky, Farrah felt a deep sense of gratitude. She had taken a leap of faith, following her heart to create a life-driven business. And in doing so, she had found not just success, but true fulfillment—a life and career as vibrant and purposeful as the art she created.

Understanding and Applying Farrah's Life-Driven Business Journey

Farrah's story offers valuable insights for anyone embarking on their own entrepreneurial journey. Let's break down the key elements of her experience and explore how you can apply them to your venture.

Integrating Your Skills and Passions

Farrah combined her project management skills, artistic talents, and passion for sustainability to create a unique business. This integration set her apart in the market.

Takeaway: Identify your skills and interests—even those unrelated to your current career. How can you combine them to create something unique? For example, if you're a teacher passionate about technology, could you develop an innovative e-learning platform?

Aligning Business with Personal Values and Lifestyle

Farrah built EcoArt MENA to align with her values and lifestyle, setting up her studio near her daughter's school and structuring work around family commitments.

Takeaway: Consider how your business idea aligns with your values and desired lifestyle. Does it support your ideal way of living? How can you structure it to fit your needs?

Starting Small and Scaling Gradually

Farrah started with small art pieces before expanding to larger installations. This approach allowed her to test and refine her model with minimal risk.

Takeaway: Start small. Test your idea with minimal risk before scaling up. Can you offer your product or service on a limited basis while maintaining your current job?

Leveraging Your Unique Perspective

Farrah's understanding of Middle Eastern culture gave her an edge in creating art that resonated with local audiences while promoting global sustainability.

Takeaway: Reflect on your unique experiences or cultural background. How can these inform your business and set you apart from competitors?

Defining Success Beyond Finances

Farrah measured success not only financially but also through her impact on environmental conservation and community education.

Takeaway: Define success beyond profit. What impact do you want to make? How can your business contribute to causes you care about?

Embracing Evolution and Growth

Farrah stayed open to new opportunities, expanding into workshops and adopting technologies like virtual reality.

Takeaway: Stay flexible. Be open to new technologies, opportunities, and evolving your business model based on market trends and customer feedback.

By understanding and applying these elements of Farrah's journey, you can create a business that aligns with your values, supports your lifestyle, and allows you to make the impact you desire. Remember, the goal is not just financial success but to build a fulfilling and purpose-driven enterprise.

Reflection Questions and Action Steps:

- **Identify Your Unique Blend**: Reflect on your skills and passions. Make a list of what you enjoy and excel at. Consider how these can be combined to create a unique business idea that stands out in the market.

- **Align Business with Lifestyle**: Think about how your business can fit into your desired lifestyle. Identify practical ways to integrate work with personal commitments, such as choosing a location convenient for family needs or setting flexible work hours.

- **Defining Personal Success**: Beyond finances, what does success look like to you? How can your business reflect your values?

- **Embracing Growth and Evolution**: How can you stay flexible and adapt to changes in your business journey?

Creating a life-driven business is a personal journey. Stay true to yourself, align your business with your evolving goals, and use these reflections to guide you toward a more fulfilling future.

Conclusion

An intentional life and business take time and consideration. Take a moment to imagine the possibilities that lie ahead. You've embarked on a journey that goes beyond traditional entrepreneurship–a path to discover the perfect blend of your passions, skills, and values into a tapestry of personal and professional fulfillment.

Remember Farrah's story, how she transformed her career from project management to sustainable art, creating a business that not only succeeds financially but also aligns perfectly with her values and lifestyle. This isn't just a story of business success; it's a testament to the power of authenticity and purpose in entrepreneurship.

By embracing the life-driven business model, you're opening doors to a world where work doesn't feel like work. Imagine waking up excited each day about the impact you're making, the creativity you're expressing, and the life you're living. This is the promise of a life-driven business, a harmony between your professional aspirations and personal fulfillment.

As you move forward, remember that this journey is uniquely yours. Your life-driven business will be as individual as your fingerprint, shaped by your experiences, skills, and dreams. Embrace this individuality, it's your greatest strength in a world that often pushes for conformity.

The path ahead may not always be easy. There will be challenges, doubts, and moments of uncertainty. But armed with the principles you've learned–integrating your skills and passions, aligning your business with your values, starting small and scaling thoughtfully, leveraging your unique perspective, and defining success on your own terms–you're well-equipped to navigate this journey.

Your life-driven business has the potential to be more than just a source of income. It can be a platform for personal growth, a vehicle for positive change in your community, and a testament to what's possible when you dare to dream differently.

So, as you close this chapter, carry with you the excitement of possibility. The world is waiting for the unique value that only you can bring. Your life-driven business isn't just a distant dream–it's a tangible future that you have the power to create.

Take that first step. Embrace your authenticity. Trust in your vision. The journey to your life-driven business starts now, and the possibilities are limitless. Your future self–fulfilled, impactful, and living life on your own terms–is counting on you to begin. The world needs your unique contribution. Are you ready to answer the call?

CHAPTER 13

Find Your Tribe

"You are the average of the five people you spend the most time with."

–Jim Rohn

The gentle clinking of wine glasses and the soft murmur of conversation filled my Dubai apartment on the 30th floor of Jumeirah Village Circle. As the clock struck 7:00 PM, the last rays of the setting sun painted the sky in hues of orange and pink, visible through the floor-to-ceiling windows that offered a breathtaking view of the city below. The cool air conditioning was a welcome respite from the lingering heat of the day, creating a comfortable atmosphere for the diverse group of women gathered in my living room.

I felt a surge of pride mixed with a twinge of nervousness as I looked around at my guests. This wasn't just any social gathering; it was my first attempt at creating a genuine support system in my adopted home. The idea had come to me after reading "The 2-Hour Cocktail Party," a book that spoke to my introverted nature and my desire for deeper, more meaningful connections in a world that often felt superficial and overwhelming.

"Ladies, thank you all for coming," I said, my voice slightly shaky as I addressed the room. "I know we're all busy, so I really appreciate you taking the time to be here tonight."

Just a few months earlier, I had been drowning in the vastness of expat life in Dubai. The initial excitement of moving to this glittering city had worn off, replaced by a gnawing loneliness that even the bustling streets and towering skyscrapers couldn't dispel. Networking events and expat mixers left me feeling drained and disconnected. The thought of navigating another crowded bar or forced small talk made me want to retreat further into my shell.

With a mix of excitement and trepidation, I had sent out invitations to a hand-picked group of women, some familiar faces, others mere acquaintances. The goal wasn't to expand my network but to deepen it, to find my tribe in this foreign land.

As we began with icebreakers, the initial awkwardness melted away. The room filled with laughter and animated conversation as each woman shared who she was, where she came from, and what she did. The diversity was striking; entrepreneurs, published authors, corporate executives, and stay-at-home moms, hailing from various corners of the globe but all united by the shared experience of building a life in Dubai.

Sarah, a British retiree, spoke of her decision to spend her golden years in the UAE, away from the familiar but seeking new adventures. "I never thought I'd end up in Dubai," she chuckled, her eyes twinkling. "But here I am, learning Arabic and loving every minute of it."

Aisha, a young Emirati entrepreneur, shared her dreams of bridging cultures through her tech startup. "It's not always easy being a woman in tech," she admitted, "but Dubai gives me opportunities I wouldn't have elsewhere."

Mei, a Chinese expat and mother of two, talked about the challenges of raising third-culture kids. "Sometimes I worry they're not Chinese enough, not Emirati enough," she sighed. "But then I realize they're citizens of the world, and that's beautiful."

As the evening progressed and we moved from structured introductions to casual conversations, I found myself drawn to two women in particular.

Amber, a vivacious blonde from Texas, stood out not just for her height but for her infectious laugh that seemed to fill the room. She was gesticulating animatedly as she spoke to a small group near the window.

"Y'all wouldn't believe the looks I get when I tell people I own a motorsport shop," she drawled, her blue eyes sparkling with amusement. "They expect some burly guy with a beard, not little ol' me."

I approached her, intrigued. "Amber, right? I'm sorry, I couldn't help overhearing. Did you say you own a motorsport shop?"

She turned to me with a warm smile. "Sure do, honey! Bikes, ATVs, you name it. Brought a little piece of Texas to the desert, you could say."

"That's incredible," I said, genuinely impressed. "How did you end up doing that in Dubai, of all places?"

Amber's eyes lit up. "Oh, it's a long story involving a canceled flight, a shawarma, and a chance meeting with a sheikh who loves Harleys. But the short version is, I saw an opportunity and grabbed it with both hands. Ain't that what being an expat is all about?"

I nodded, feeling a connection forming. "It certainly is. The courage to take risks, to build something new..."

"Exactly!" Amber exclaimed, patting my arm. "And let me tell you, it ain't always easy. But nights like this, meeting other women who are out here hustling and making their dreams come true? That's what keeps me going."

As Amber and I chatted, I noticed a younger woman hovering nearby, seemingly wanting to join the conversation but hesitant to interrupt. I caught her eye and smiled encouragingly.

"Please, join us," I said, gesturing her over. "I don't think we've been properly introduced. I'm the host, and this is Amber."

The young woman stepped forward, her perfectly applied makeup accentuating her striking features. "I'm Nikita," she said, her voice soft but clear. "It's so nice to meet you both. I hope I'm not interrupting."

"Not at all, sugar," Amber said warmly. "We were just talking about our journeys here in Dubai. What's your story?"

Nikita's eyes lit up. "Well, I'm a makeup artist. I moved here from Mumbai about two years ago, chasing my dream of working in the beauty industry."

"A makeup artist?" I echoed, intrigued. "That must be fascinating work, especially here in Dubai."

Nikita nodded enthusiastically. "Oh, it is! The diversity here is incredible. One day I'm doing traditional Arabic makeup for a wedding, the next I'm creating avant-garde looks for a fashion show. It's challenging, but I love it."

"Sounds like you're living your dream," Amber said approvingly. "But I bet it ain't always easy, being young and on your own in a new city."

A shadow passed over Nikita's face. "It can be lonely sometimes," she admitted. "I love my work, but I don't have many close friends here yet. That's why I was so excited to come tonight."

I felt a surge of empathy. "I know exactly how you feel, Nikita. That's actually why I organized this gathering. I was hoping to create deeper connections, to find people who could understand the unique challenges of expat life."

Amber nodded sagely. "Y'all are speaking my language. It's one thing to be successful in your work, but it's another to have people who really get you, who can be there for you through the ups and downs."

As the evening wore on, I found myself gravitating back to Amber and Nikita time and again. Despite our different backgrounds and ages, there was an easy camaraderie between us. We shared stories of culture shock, of homesickness, of small triumphs and embarrassing faux pas.

"Remember, ladies," Amber said at one point, raising her glass, "we're all pioneers here. We're building lives in a place our grandmamas probably never even heard of. That takes guts, and it takes heart."

Nikita nodded, her eyes shining. "And it takes support. I'm so grateful to have met you both tonight. It's... it's like finding family."

As the clock approached 9:00 PM and guests began to say goodbyes, Amber and Nikita lingered. We exchanged numbers, made plans to meet for coffee the following week.

"This was just wonderful," Amber said, giving me a warm hug. "You've started something special here, honey. Count me in for the next one."

Nikita echoed the sentiment. "Thank you so much for organizing this. I haven't felt this... seen in a long time."

As I closed the door behind the last guest, I leaned against it, feeling a warmth in my chest that had nothing to do with the Dubai heat. The evening had exceeded my wildest hopes. Not only had I made connections, but I felt I had found kindred spirits in Amber and Nikita.

In the weeks and months that followed, those connections deepened. We celebrated each other's successes, consoled each other through setbacks. Amber's can-do spirit and Nikita's youthful enthusiasm became a constant sources of inspiration and support.

One day, as we sat in a café, sharing news and dreams over steaming cups of karak chai, I realized something profound. In this glittering city of gold and glass, I had found something far more precious; a cheerleading squad, a support system, a chosen family.

Building a life abroad is never easy. But with the right people by your side, people who understand your journey, who lift you up and cheer you on, it becomes an adventure worth every challenge. And it all started with a simple gathering, a leap of faith, and the courage to open my home and my heart to new connections.

Rule: Build an Emotional Safety Net Abroad

In the challenging world of expat entrepreneurship, there's a golden rule that can make the difference between merely surviving and truly thriving: Build an Emotional Safety Net Abroad. This isn't just about casual networking or making fair-weather friends. It's about intentionally cultivating a support system that understands and nurtures your emotional well-being in a foreign land, acting as your anchor in the stormy seas of cultural adjustment and entrepreneurial challenges.

This rule is about creating a small, tight-knit group of individuals who become your 'cheerleading squad' abroad. These are the people who will check in on you regularly, not just about your business ventures, but about your overall well-being. They're the ones who'll ask if you've eaten a proper meal, if you've stepped outside for some fresh air today, if you're getting enough sleep. They become your emotional anchors, your sounding boards, and your home away from home.

Why It's Crucial

Entrepreneurship, by its very nature, is an emotional rollercoaster. Now, imagine riding that rollercoaster in a foreign country, far from your usual support systems of family and lifelong friends. Every up feels higher, every down feels lower, and the twists and turns of cultural differences add an extra layer of complexity to the ride.

This rule recognizes a fundamental truth: your emotional health is not just a personal matter, it's a critical business asset. Just as you wouldn't neglect your financial capital, you can't afford to neglect your emotional capital. Your ability to weather storms, seize opportunities, and lead effectively all stems from a foundation of emotional well-being.

Moreover, as expats, we often feel pressure to project an image of effortless success. We want to prove to ourselves and others that we can make it on our own in a new country. This rule challenges that notion, acknowledging that true strength lies in vulnerability and interdependence, not in isolation and false bravado.

The Multifaceted Benefits of Following This Rule

1. **Emotional Resilience**: Building an emotional safety net provides you with a buffer against the inevitable setbacks and challenges of expat life and entrepreneurship. When you have people who truly understand your journey, you're better equipped to bounce back from failures, navigate cultural misunderstandings, and maintain a positive outlook, even in tough times. This emotional resilience isn't just about feeling better, it translates directly into business resilience. You'll be more likely to persevere through tough times, pivot when necessary, and maintain the long-term vision needed for success.

2. **Mental Health Preservation**: Expat life can be isolating, and entrepreneurship can be stressful. Combined, they can create a perfect storm for mental health issues. Your emotional safety net acts as a preventative measure against depression, anxiety, and burnout. Regular check-ins with your support group can help you recognize early signs of mental health struggles. They can encourage you to seek professional help if needed, or simply provide a listening ear during tough times. This

proactive approach to mental health can save you from major setbacks down the line.

3. **Physical Health Benefits**: Your emotional safety net doesn't just care about your feelings, they care about your overall well-being. They're the ones who'll remind you to eat properly, to get enough sleep, to exercise regularly. In the hustle of entrepreneurship, it's easy to neglect these basic needs, but your support system won't let you. This focus on physical health has direct benefits for your business. Better physical health means more energy, better cognitive function, and increased productivity. You'll be able to work smarter, not just harder.

4. **Work-Life Balance**: One of the biggest challenges for expat entrepreneurs is maintaining a healthy work-life balance. Without the usual structures of home, it's easy to fall into the trap of all work and no play. Your emotional safety net can help you maintain perspective. They'll remind you to take breaks, to explore your new country, to engage in hobbies and relaxation. This balance isn't just good for you personally—it's good for business. Time away from work can lead to fresh insights, creative solutions, and renewed energy for your entrepreneurial endeavors.

5. **Reciprocal Help and Personal Growth**: Building an emotional safety net isn't just about receiving support, it's also about giving it. As you help others in your circle, you'll find that you're growing too. You'll develop greater empathy, improve your communication skills, and gain new perspectives. This reciprocal flow creates a virtuous cycle. As you support others, you'll find yourself more connected and valued. This sense of belonging can be a powerful antidote to the feelings of isolation that often accompany expat life.

6. **Time Efficiency and Real-Time Feedback**: Your emotional safety net can serve as an invaluable sounding board for your ideas and decisions. They can provide real-time feedback, helping you catch potential mistakes before they become costly, or identify opportunities you might have missed. This real-time feedback loop can save you significant time

and resources. Instead of learning everything through trial and error, you can benefit from the collective wisdom and experience of your support network.

7. **Cultural Integration**: Your emotional safety net, especially if it includes locals or long-term expats, can accelerate your cultural integration. They can help you navigate cultural nuances, understand unwritten social rules, and appreciate the subtleties of your new home. This deeper cultural understanding isn't just personally enriching—it can be a significant business advantage. It can help you better understand local markets, connect with local customers, and avoid cultural faux pas that could harm your business.

8. **Encouragement and Motivation**: Perhaps one of the most powerful benefits of your emotional safety net is the constant source of encouragement and motivation they provide. In the world of entrepreneurship, where self-doubt can be crippling, having a group of people who believe in you can make all the difference. This encouragement can help you push through tough times, celebrate small wins, and maintain the motivation needed for long-term success. It's like having your own personal cheering squad, always ready to boost your spirits and remind you of your capabilities.

The Consequences of Neglecting This Rule

Failing to build your emotional safety net can lead to a host of negative outcomes:

- **Burnout**: Without someone to notice the signs of overwork, you might push yourself beyond your limits.

- **Isolation**: The initial excitement of a new country can wear off, leaving you feeling alone and disconnected.

- **Poor Decision Making**: Stress and emotional turmoil can cloud your judgment in both personal and business matters.

- **Health Issues**: Neglecting your physical and mental health can lead to serious problems that can derail your entrepreneurial journey.

- **Cultural Missteps**: Without guidance, you might inadvertently make cultural mistakes that could harm your business or personal relationships.

- **Giving Up**: In the face of challenges, without support, you might be more likely to throw in the towel and head home, abandoning your entrepreneurial dreams.

The Bigger Picture

This rule is about more than just feeling good or having friends. It's a strategic approach to expat entrepreneurship that recognizes the inextricable link between emotional well-being and business success. By prioritizing the creation of a strong support system, you're not just surviving abroad—you're setting yourself up to thrive.

Remember, in the journey of expat entrepreneurship, your emotional resilience is as crucial as your business acumen. Your support system isn't a luxury, it's a necessity. It's the invisible structure that holds you up when things get tough, celebrates with you in times of triumph, and keeps you grounded throughout the rollercoaster ride of building a life and business abroad.

By following this rule and building your emotional safety net, you're not just creating a business, you're crafting a fulfilling, sustainable life in your new home. You're creating a support structure that allows you to take bigger risks, bounce back from failures, learn and grow continuously, and fully embrace the incredible adventure of being an expat entrepreneur. In doing so, you're ensuring that your expat journey is rich, rewarding, and deeply meaningful on both a personal and professional level.

CASE STUDY: THANDI'S TECH STARTUP IN DUBAI

Thandi, a 28-year-old marketing professional from Cape Town, had always dreamed of building her own tech startup. When an opportunity arose to join a prestigious firm in Dubai, she saw it as a stepping stone towards her entrepreneurial goals. With a mix of excitement and trepidation, she packed her bags and set off for the glittering city in the desert.

The Initial Struggle

The first few months in Dubai were a whirlwind. Thandi was amazed by the city's towering skyscrapers, luxurious malls, and diverse population. However, the initial excitement soon gave way to the harsh realities of expat life.

Her job, while rewarding, demanded long hours. It wasn't uncommon for Thandi to arrive at the office before sunrise and leave well after sunset. The pressure to perform in a highly competitive environment was intense, and she often worked weekends to meet deadlines.

Outside of work, Thandi threw herself into the startup scene. She joined several tech groups and women's entrepreneurship circles, hoping to network and develop her business ideas. However, she found these connections lacking the depth she craved.

One evening, after an uninspiring networking event, Thandi called her sister back in Cape Town.

"I don't get it, Lulu," Thandi sighed. "I'm meeting so many people, but I feel more alone than ever."

Her sister's voice crackled over the line, "What do you mean, Thandi? Aren't you always telling me about these events you're going to?"

Thandi flopped onto her couch, staring at the twinkling Dubai skyline outside her window. "Yeah, but it's all so... superficial. Everyone's either trying to sell something or looking for their next job. People come and go so quickly here. Just when I think I've made a friend, they're off to their next expat adventure."

"Oh," Lulu said softly. "That sounds tough. What about the women's groups you joined?"

Thandi sighed again. "Same thing. We talk about business strategies and funding, which is great, but... I don't know. I guess I'm missing that personal connection. Someone to just be real with, you know?"

The Turning Point

After hanging up, Thandi sat in silence, reflecting on the conversation. She realized that while she was pursuing her professional dreams, she was neglecting her emotional needs.

The next day at work, Thandi overheard a colleague, Aisha, talking about feeling homesick.

"Hey, Aisha," Thandi said, approaching her. "I couldn't help overhearing. I've been feeling the same way lately."

Aisha looked surprised, then relieved. "Really? I thought it was just me. Everyone always seems so put together here."

Thandi laughed. "Trust me, we're all just pretending. Listen, I have an idea. Why don't we have a small get-together this weekend? Just a few people, nothing fancy. We could all use some proper conversation."

Aisha's face lit up. "That sounds wonderful! Can I invite my roommate? She's new here too."

"Of course," Thandi smiled. "The more, the merrier."

The Gathering

That Saturday evening, Thandi's small apartment was filled with the sounds of conversation and laughter. She had invited Aisha and her roommate, a couple of other colleagues, and a few acquaintances from her various networking groups.

As they shared food and stories, Thandi opened up about her struggles and her entrepreneurial dreams.

"I just feel like I'm constantly networking, but never actually connecting," Thandi admitted to the group.

To her amazement, many of her guests nodded in understanding.

"Oh my god, yes!" exclaimed Sarah, a British expat Thandi had met at a tech meetup. "I thought I was the only one who felt that way. It's like everyone's on LinkedIn 24/7 here."

Priya, an Indian software engineer, chimed in. "I've been here for three years, and let me tell you, it gets better. But you have to be intentional about building real friendships."

As the night went on, the conversation flowed from work challenges to dating woes to homesickness. Thandi felt a weight lifting off her shoulders. For the first time in months, she didn't feel alone in her struggles.

The Aftermath

As the evening wound down, Thandi pulled Aisha aside. "Thank you for coming. This meant more to me than you know."

Aisha hugged her. "Thank you for organizing it. We should do this regularly, don't you think?"

Thandi nodded enthusiastically. "Absolutely. Maybe we can rotate hosts?"

In the weeks that followed, Thandi noticed significant changes:

1. The group created a WhatsApp chat where they shared everything from funny memes to advice on dealing with difficult bosses and potential investors.

2. Thandi started taking lunch breaks, often brainstorming startup ideas with Sarah, who had experience in tech entrepreneurship.

3. On particularly stressful days, she now had people she could call for a quick pep talk or a listening ear.

4. Weekends became more than just recovery time. She started exploring Dubai with her new friends, finally enjoying the city she'd moved to.

5. With encouragement from her support group, Thandi set boundaries at work, learning to say no to unreasonable demands on her time.

6. Her physical health improved as Priya introduced her to a great yoga studio that offered sunrise classes.

The Outcome

Six months after that first gathering, Thandi's life in Dubai looked markedly different. While she still worked hard at her day job, she had also made progress on her startup idea, with support and feedback from her new friends.

One evening, as Thandi was preparing to host another get-together, she received a call from Lulu.

"Hey, how are you doing?" Lulu asked.

Thandi smiled, realizing how different she felt compared to their last call. "I'm doing really well, actually. Remember how lonely I was feeling?"

"Of course. You sounded so down."

"Well, things have changed. I took your advice about making real connections. I've found my people here, Lulu. They support me, challenge me, and remind me to take care of myself. It's made all the difference."

Lulu's voice was warm with happiness. "Oh, Thandi, that's wonderful! Tell me all about it."

As Thandi shared her story, she realized that building this emotional safety net hadn't just improved her personal life, it had given her the support and confidence she needed to pursue her entrepreneurial dreams. She was more focused, more creative, and better able to handle the pressures of both her job and her startup aspirations.

Looking back, Thandi recognized that simple gathering was a turning point in her expat journey. By reaching out and building genuine connections, she had transformed her experience in Dubai from one of isolation and burnout to one of growth, balance, and fulfillment. She had found her cheerleading squad, and with their support, she felt ready to take on any challenge Dubai could throw at her.

Examining Thandi's Story: Applying the Rule

Thandi's experience in Dubai illustrates how the rule "Build Your Emotional Safety Net Abroad" can be applied in real life. Let's examine how her actions aligned with this rule and the resulting impact on her expat journey.

Recognizing the Need

The first step in applying the rule is recognizing the need for an emotional safety net. Initially, Thandi struggled with this. She immersed herself in work and networking events, believing that professional connections would fulfill her needs. However, she soon realized that these superficial interactions left her feeling empty and isolated. This realization was crucial, it pushed her to seek more meaningful connections.

Taking Initiative

Once Thandi recognized her need for deeper relationships, she created opportunities for connection. By organizing a small gathering in her apartment, she actively applied the rule's principle of intentionally cultivating a support system. This showed courage and vulnerability, two key components in building genuine relationships.

Creating a Safe Space

Thandi's decision to host the gathering in her home was significant. It created an intimate, relaxed environment where people felt comfortable opening up. This aligns with the rule's emphasis on creating spaces where vulnerability is encouraged and genuine connections can form.

Encouraging Openness

During the gathering, Thandi shared her own struggles and aspirations. By doing so, she set a tone of openness and authenticity. This encouraged others to reciprocate, leading to more meaningful conversations and connections. This mirrors the rule's emphasis on the power of vulnerability in forming strong bonds.

Consistency and Follow-Through

Thandi and her new friends made their gatherings a regular event. This consistency is crucial in applying the rule effectively. Building an emotional safety net isn't a onetime event but an ongoing process of nurturing relationships.

Mutual Support

The WhatsApp group that emerged from these gatherings exemplifies the day-to-day support system the rule advocates for. It provided a platform for constant connection, allowing Thandi and her friends to share both triumphs and challenges, offer encouragement, and provide practical help.

Holistic Well-being

As Thandi's support network grew, she saw improvements in various aspects of her life. She started taking better care of her physical health, set healthier boundaries at work, and found renewed energy for her entrepreneurial pursuits. This holistic improvement aligns with the rule's assertion that an emotional safety net benefits all areas of life.

Professional Growth

Interestingly, by focusing on building personal connections rather than just professional networks, Thandi ultimately found more support for her career goals. Her new friends provided not just emotional support but also practical advice and encouragement for her entrepreneurial dreams. This demonstrates the rule's principle that emotional well-being and professional success are interconnected.

Cultural Integration

Through her new friendships, Thandi began to explore and enjoy Dubai more fully. This increased cultural integration is another benefit the rule promises, a deeper connection to your new home through genuine relationships with others.

Long-term Impact

Six months after applying this rule, Thandi's expat experience had transformed dramatically. She had found her "cheerleading squad"–a group of people who supported her emotionally, encouraged her professionally, and enriched her life in Dubai. This long-term positive impact is exactly what the rule "Build Your Emotional Safety Net Abroad" promises.

In conclusion, Thandi's story vividly illustrates the power of intentionally building an emotional safety net abroad. By recognizing her need for deeper connections, taking initiative, creating safe spaces for vulnerability, maintaining consistency, and embracing mutual support, Thandi successfully applied the rule to her life. The result was a richer, more fulfilling expat experience that supported both her personal well-being and her professional aspirations. Her journey serves as a testament to the transformative power of building a strong emotional support system in a foreign land.

Take a Moment to Reflect

Now it's time to turn the lens on your own experience. Whether you're currently living abroad, planning an international move, or simply considering the possibility, these questions will help you reflect on your own emotional support system and identify areas for potential growth.

Reflection Questions:

Take a moment to consider each question carefully. Be honest with yourself–this reflection is for your benefit, to help you create a more fulfilling and balanced life abroad.

- Who do you turn to when you need emotional support in your daily life as an expat? How satisfied are you with the depth and quality of your current relationships in your host country? Do you have people in your life who truly understand your expat journey and its unique challenges?

- How comfortable do you feel being vulnerable with others in your current environment? When was the last time you had a truly authentic conversation about your struggles or fears as an expat? Are there aspects of your expat experience you feel you can't share with anyone? If so, why?

- Consider the barriers that might prevent you from forming deeper connections. Are you holding back out of fear, cultural differences, or simply lack of opportunity?

- How proactive are you in seeking out and maintaining meaningful relationships in your host country?

- Have you ever organized a gathering similar to Thandi's? If not, what's holding you back?

- Are there communities or groups in your area that align with your interests but you haven't yet engaged with?

- How would you describe the balance between your professional and personal relationships in your host country?

- Do you feel your networking efforts are yielding the deep, supportive relationships you need?

- Are there ways you could leverage your professional networks to build more personal connections?

- Reflect on whether you're prioritizing professional connections at the expense of personal ones. How might you strike a better balance?

Remember, building an emotional safety net is an ongoing process. It requires intention, effort, and often, stepping out of your comfort zone. But as Thandi's story illustrates, the rewards–in terms of personal fulfillment, professional success, and overall well-being–can be truly transformative.

Take these questions with you as you navigate your expat journey. Revisit them regularly and use them as a guide to continuously strengthen and expand your emotional safety net. Your future self will thank you for the rich, supportive community you're building today.

Action Steps:

As we conclude this chapter on building your emotional safety net abroad, it's crucial to move from understanding to action. Reflect on your current situation and consider how you can apply what you've learned. To help you get started, here are three concrete steps you can take:

- **Host a "Connection Gathering"**: Organize a small get-together, similar to Thandi's, inviting 5-7 people you'd like to know better. This could be a mix of colleagues, neighbors, or acquaintances from various expat or local groups. The goal is to create an intimate setting where people feel comfortable opening up and sharing their experiences. Plan some icebreaker questions to get the conversation flowing, and be prepared to share your own challenges and joys as an expat.

- **Vulnerability Challenge**: Challenge yourself to have one authentic, vulnerable conversation each week with someone in your host country. This could involve sharing a struggle you're facing, asking for help with something, or expressing a fear or insecurity about your expat experience. Remember, vulnerability is a powerful tool for building genuine connections. It might feel uncomfortable at first, but it often leads to deeper, more meaningful relationships.

- **Expat Journal and Reach-Out List**: Start an "expat journal" where you regularly note your experiences, challenges, and needs. Each week, identify one item you could use support with and reach out to someone about it. This practice not only helps you process your experiences but also encourages you to actively seek support when you need it. It can also help you identify patterns in your expat journey and track your progress in building your emotional safety net.

By taking these steps, you're actively working to create the support system you need to thrive in your new home. Remember, building an emotional safety net is an ongoing process that requires intention and effort. Be patient with yourself and celebrate each small victory along the way. Your future self will thank you for the rich, supportive community you're building today.

Weaving Your Own Web of Support

Thandi's pivot was powerful. She went from feeling isolated and overwhelmed to finding a sense of belonging and support is a powerful testament to the impact of intentionally building an emotional safety net. Like Thandi, you too have the power to create a nurturing community around you, no matter where in the world you find yourself.

We've learned that this process requires courage; the courage to be vulnerable, to reach out, and to open your heart to new connections. It's about creating spaces where authentic conversations can flourish, where struggles can be shared without judgment, and where celebrations, big and small, are heartily embraced.

Building your emotional safety net isn't just about having people to turn to in times of need. It's about enriching your entire expat experience. It's about having friends who'll introduce you to hidden local gems, who'll help you navigate cultural nuances, and who'll make your new country feel more like home. It's about creating a support system that bolsters both your personal well-being and your professional aspirations.

As you step forward from this chapter, armed with strategies and action steps, remember that every great journey begins with a single step. Your first connection gathering, your first vulnerable conversation, or your first journal entry–these are the seeds from which your robust support network will grow.

Embrace this process with optimism and patience. Building meaningful relationships takes time, but the rewards are immeasurable. Picture yourself a year from now, surrounded by a diverse group of friends who truly understand and support you. Imagine the sense of belonging, the shared laughter, the mutual encouragement.

You have within you everything you need to create this reality. Your unique experiences, your openness to new connections, and your willingness to support others are all valuable threads in the tapestry of your new community.

So step out with confidence. Reach out with an open heart. Your emotional safety net awaits, ready to be woven. The rich, fulfilling expat life you dream of is not just possible–with your emotional safety net in place, it's inevitable. Your adventure in true connection starts now.

CHAPTER 14

Grow Without Burnout

"Take care of your body. It's the only place you have to live."
–Jim Rohn

I used to love the taste of a warm latte—creamy, smooth, and just sweet enough to keep me going. It became part of my daily routine. Every morning after dropping the kids off at school, I would make my way to a trendy coworking space, the kind with exposed brick walls, quirky art, and the endless hum of other ambitious entrepreneurs tapping away at their laptops.

The barista knew me by name. "Your usual, Jamilia?"

I smiled, nodding. "Yep, double shot today, please."

With my latte in hand, I'd sit down, open my laptop, and the race against the clock would begin. Emails, meetings, client calls, more emails. I told myself I was doing it—building my business, making moves. But somewhere between the endless cups of coffee and the constant grind, I stopped feeling like myself. I wasn't present with my family anymore.

By noon, I'd squeeze in a punishing gym session, like I had something to prove. I'd push myself hard—weights, cardio, anything to feel like I was still in control.

But it was never enough. Despite the workouts, I was gaining weight, feeling sluggish, and barely keeping up. After the gym, it was back to the coworking space, back to the lattes.

Every day blurred into the next. I'd leave the coworking space in the evening, feeling drained, my mind buzzing but my body worn out. I'd pick up the kids, head home, and try to be present with my husband, but I had nothing left in the tank. I'd sit with them, but my mind was elsewhere—already thinking about tomorrow's workload, tomorrow's grind. And Nemanja noticed.

One evening, after I'd spent another day on caffeine-fueled autopilot, Nemanja stopped me as I set down my laptop at the dinner table.

"Jamilia," he said, his voice gentle but firm, "you don't look like yourself anymore."

I paused, my hands still on the laptop, blinking up at him. "What do you mean?" I asked, though I already knew the answer.

He sat down across from me, leaning forward. "You're always working, always at that coworking space, drinking those lattes. You're at the gym but... you don't seem happy. You're tired all the time."

I sighed, leaning back in my chair, my shoulders sagging. He was right. My clothes didn't fit the same anymore. I didn't feel good in my own skin. "I'm trying to keep up, Nemanja. It's just... everything feels so out of balance. I'm working harder than ever, but I have no energy left for myself—let alone for you, or the kids."

Nemanja looked at me, his eyes softening. "Is it really worth it? Your health? Us? Your happiness?"

His words hit me like a wave. I sat there, staring at my laptop, the screen still glowing. I had been chasing this idea of success so relentlessly—building my business, pushing my limits—that I hadn't stopped to ask myself if it was sustainable. And the truth was, it wasn't. I was running on caffeine, adrenaline, and sheer willpower, and none of it was enough anymore. Not for my business. Not for my family. Not for me.

The next morning, I made a decision. I skipped my usual latte and opted for water instead. I still went to the coworking space, but this time, I brought a small notebook, not just my laptop. I worked, yes, but I also made time to sit by myself, away from the screen. I walked down to the beach—no phone, no emails—just the sound of the waves and the space to breathe.

I noticed a difference immediately. Instead of forcing myself through exhausting workouts, I chose activities that felt good—like yoga, walking, and swimming. It wasn't about killing myself at the gym anymore; it was about moving in a way that energized me, not drained me.

I cut back on the caffeine and started paying attention to what my body needed. I realized that what I needed most was rest—real rest. And so, I made weekends sacred again. No more laptops, no more work late into the night. I gave myself permission to unplug, to enjoy my family without feeling guilty.

And it changed everything.

I was more creative, more focused. Ideas flowed naturally, and my business started to grow in ways I hadn't expected. I stopped grinding just to survive and started thriving. I realized that rest isn't something you earn after success—it's a critical part of being successful.

One evening, a few weeks after I'd started making these changes, Nemanja looked at me from across the dinner table and smiled. "You're different," he said, his eyes warm.

I smiled back. "Yeah… I feel different."

I had finally found the balance I needed, and it was more than just physical. It was mental, emotional, and it made me a better entrepreneur, a better wife, and a better mother. Success wasn't about burning myself out anymore. It was about showing up as the best version of me.

And that's when everything changed.

The Rule: Balancing Business Growth with Personal Well-Being

As an expat entrepreneur, it's easy to get swept up in the demands of running and growing your business. However, sustained growth requires more than just hard work—it requires balance. The most successful and resilient businesses are built on a foundation of personal well-being, where the entrepreneur thrives mentally, physically, and emotionally. This rule emphasizes the need to integrate your personal wellness into your business strategy, creating a sustainable path to long-term success.

Work-Life Integration, Not Work-Life Separation

Rather than trying to separate work and personal life into distinct categories, successful entrepreneurs learn to integrate the two. Work-life *integration* means allowing both your professional and personal goals to coexist in harmony. This involves:

- Designing your business model to allow flexibility and downtime for personal activities.

- Structuring your daily schedule so that wellness practices—such as exercise, meditation, or even family time—are non-negotiable parts of your routine.

- Ensuring that your personal values and lifestyle choices are reflected in your business. If you value travel, for example, your business should allow location independence.

This shift from work-life separation to work-life integration is essential for expats, who often face unique challenges abroad, such as cultural adaptation, isolation, and managing different time zones. Instead of viewing wellness as something you do *outside* of business hours, incorporate it into your workday to create a seamless flow between the two.

Mental Health is a Business Asset

Many entrepreneurs underestimate the importance of mental clarity and emotional resilience. Yet, when mental health is neglected, it directly affects decision-making, creativity, and overall productivity. To sustain growth in your business, you must protect your mental well-being just as you would any other critical asset in your company.

Key practices include:

- **Mindfulness and Meditation**: Incorporating mindfulness practices into your daily routine helps manage stress, improve focus, and increase emotional resilience. Even 10-15 minutes a day can help you stay grounded and clear-headed amidst business challenges.

- **Stress Management**: Recognize the early signs of burnout—such as irritability, fatigue, or a constant feeling of being overwhelmed—and take proactive steps to manage stress. This could mean taking regular breaks, engaging in hobbies, or spending time in nature to recharge.

- **Emotional Regulation**: Business often involves high-pressure situations. By developing emotional regulation techniques—such as deep breathing, journaling, or talking with a coach or therapist—you can approach these situations calmly and with better judgment.

Your mental health is as much a business asset as your financial capital. The clearer your mind, the better your decisions and, ultimately, your business outcomes.

Physical Health Fuels Business Success

Entrepreneurs often underestimate how physical health impacts their business performance. Energy, stamina, and cognitive function are all tied to your physical well-being. A healthy body allows you to bring your best self to your business, deciding with clarity and executing strategies with focus.

Steps to prioritize physical health include:

- **Daily Movement**: Whether it's a morning run, yoga, or even a brisk walk, moving your body daily helps increase energy, reduce stress, and improve focus. Find a routine that works for you, especially considering the different environments you might find yourself in as an expat.

- **Nutrition**: Fueling your body with nutritious food ensures sustained energy levels throughout the day. As an expat, you may have access to new and exotic foods—use this as an opportunity to discover healthy local cuisines that can nourish your body while respecting local traditions.

- **Rest and Recovery**: Rest is essential for maintaining long-term productivity. Prioritize quality sleep and take time off when needed. Consider "work sprints" followed by downtime, or schedule vacation periods to reset your mind and body.

By prioritizing your physical health, you're not only ensuring that you'll have the energy to scale your business, but also that you'll be mentally sharp enough to make critical decisions along the way.

Shifting the Mindset: Wellness as a Growth Strategy

Entrepreneurs often think that taking care of themselves is a luxury that can be deferred in favor of business demands. However, in reality, wellness is a *growth strategy*. When you invest in yourself, you're also investing in your business.

This requires a mindset shift:

- **Wellness First, Business Second**: This isn't about ignoring your business responsibilities, but understanding that the foundation of long-term business growth is a healthy, well-functioning you.

- **Rethink Hustle Culture**: Many entrepreneurs abroad, especially expats, feel a pressure to overwork, often due to being in unfamiliar environments or needing to prove themselves. However, constantly pushing without rest diminishes creativity and productivity. Instead of hustling non-stop, balance periods of intense focus with times of rest.

- **Sustainable Scaling**: As you grow your business, factor in your well-being. Sustainable scaling involves building your business at a pace that allows you to maintain personal health, rather than sacrificing yourself in the process. This could mean hiring help, delegating tasks, or automating parts of your business to free up time for wellness.

By shifting your mindset and viewing personal wellness as integral to business success, you ensure that both you and your business can thrive long term.

CASE STUDY: MATT'S WAKE-UP CALL

Matt stared at the glowing screen of his phone, scrolling through LinkedIn as he downed another can of energy drink. His latest post—a photo of him standing in front of a packed conference hall in Tokyo—was racking up likes. "Crushing it at the Global Tech Summit," he had written. The notifications kept pinging, each one a small hit of validation.

"Maybe I'll hit 10,000 views this time," he muttered, sipping the last of the drink and tossing the empty can into the growing pile next to his desk.

It was already 2 AM in Singapore, but Matt didn't care. He had another call with a client in London in an hour, followed by a meeting to finalize details for a product launch in Hong Kong. His calendar was a blur of meetings, launches, and flights to different corners of the world. Sleep was a luxury he couldn't afford, not with the pace he had set for himself.

His phone buzzed, and he saw a message from his business partner:

"Great dinner tonight! Hope you got home safe. Ready for tomorrow's pitch? 9 AM sharp!"

Matt sighed, leaning back in his chair, his muscles aching. He had just returned from yet another late-night dinner with potential investors—too much wine, too many drinks, but he had to show up, didn't he? That's what success looked like: being everywhere, always on, always *hustling*.

"Yeah, sure. Let's get it," he texted back, his fingers heavy. He rubbed his eyes, trying to ignore the throbbing headache creeping in. A small voice in the back of his mind whispered, *You can't keep doing this*. But he silenced it, as he always did, telling himself that this was what it took to succeed.

A few days later, in a hotel lobby in Shanghai, Matt felt disconnected during a product demo. As he smiled through the presentation, nodding along with the client's questions, his vision blurred slightly, and his heart raced. He gripped the edge of the table, willing himself to focus.

Not now, he thought, swallowing hard. The meeting ended, and his client shook his hand, grinning as if nothing had happened.

"Great work, Matt. I'll follow up with the contract next week," the client said, turning to leave.

Matt forced a smile. "Looking forward to it," he replied, his voice tight, but inside he felt like he was drowning.

Once the client left, Matt stumbled to the nearest chair and collapsed into it. His pulse was pounding, his breath shallow.

What the hell is happening to me? he wondered, clutching his chest as he tried to calm down. It wasn't the first time he'd felt this way, but it was the first time the fear gripped him so hard. He had been brushing off these episodes for weeks now—the dizziness, the pounding heart, the nights spent awake, wired but exhausted.

His phone buzzed again, and he glanced down. Another message from his partner, "Remember, we've got a team dinner tonight. Don't bail, man!"

Matt stared at the screen, his head spinning. He knew he couldn't keep going like this, but the thought of slowing down terrified him.

That night, after yet another social dinner with clients, Matt lay on the cold floor of his apartment, his heart hammering, his body trembling. The room was dark except for the dim glow of his laptop, still open on the couch where he had left it.

He had collapsed the moment he walked in the door, the weight of exhaustion finally too much to bear. His muscles felt like lead, and his head throbbed from the constant stream of energy drinks, caffeine, and alcohol that had kept him going for months. Tears pricked at his eyes, but he forced them back, staring blankly at the ceiling.

"What the hell am I doing?" he whispered to himself, his voice barely audible.

He felt so far from everything that mattered. His family, back in California, hadn't seen him in nearly a year. They called now and then, but he was always too busy to talk. His mother had left him a voicemail just a few days ago, her voice full of concern, *"Matt, honey, you sound tired. Are you okay? Call me when you get a minute."*

But there was never a minute.

His phone buzzed again, and he glanced at the screen through blurry eyes. This time, it was a photo from a friend back home—a group of them smiling and laughing at a barbecue. *Wish you were here, man,* the caption read.

Matt clenched his jaw, a wave of frustration washing over him. He had traded all of that—family, friends, peace of mind—for a business that was eating him alive. His body felt like it was falling apart, and mentally, he was hanging on by a thread.

This isn't success. This is killing me, he thought. And for the first time, he allowed himself to feel the truth of it.

Are you in Balance?

As entrepreneurs, especially expats building businesses abroad, the drive for success can be overwhelming. Matt's story is a powerful reminder that even when everything seems to go right from the outside, there can be a storm brewing within. It's easy to get caught up because success means constantly doing more—more meetings, more travel, more social engagements—but at what cost?

Reflect on the warning signs Matt experienced: the sleepless nights, the constant fatigue, the physical collapse. These are not rare experiences for entrepreneurs, especially those working in unfamiliar environments. The challenge of adapting to new cultures and time zones while managing a growing business can feel relentless. It's tempting to push yourself harder, to sacrifice sleep, health, and personal time in pursuit of that next business milestone.

But what happens when your body and mind simply can't keep up anymore? Matt's wake-up call is a reminder that balance is not just a nice-to-have—it's essential for long-term success. Burnout is real, and it doesn't just affect your health—it affects your ability to lead, to think creatively, and to sustain your business growth over time.

Take a moment to reflect on your own life. Are there areas where you're sacrificing too much for your business? How are you prioritizing your mental and physical health? Success isn't just about how much you can achieve—it's about how well you can maintain a balanced, fulfilling life while growing your business. How can you make that shift today?

Work–Life Integration Plan: Old Me vs. New Me

Old Me	New Me

How to Do This Exercise

- **Identify "Old Me" habits**: Think of habits or routines that you currently practice that throw you out of balance. "Old Me" habits are habits that are unhealthy, decrease productivity, or steal your joy. These can be small habits like eating cookies before bed, or zoning out in your phone to distract you from problems. Write as many of these as you can in the "Old Me" column.

- **Replace the "Old Me" habits with "New Me" habits**: For every "Old Me" habit that pushes out of balance, there as to be a new habit that can put you back in balance. Instead of eating cookies before bed, consider eating a high-protein alternative like Greek yogurt. Instead of doom scrolling, consider mindful breathing and meditation. Go through your list and knock out those old habits with new habits that get you back in balance.

- **Choose 2-3 changes**: Reflect on all of the habits and pick two to three habits that you are willing to work on. Make sure you choose something that you can commit to and be consistent with.

- **Commit to Progress**: Journal or track these changes daily, paying attention to how they impact your energy levels, mood, and productivity. Do this for 30 days at least.

- **Celebrate**: At the end of 30 days, celebrate your wins. You did this!

Get in Balance for Sustainability

Finding the balance between business growth and personal well-being is essential for long-term success, especially as an expat entrepreneur. Matt's story shows that the relentless hustle can only take you so far before your body and mind demand attention. Prioritizing work-life integration, taking care of your physical and mental health, and setting boundaries are not just about avoiding burnout—they are about building a sustainable foundation for both your business and your life.

As you move forward, remember that success is not defined by how much you can sacrifice, but by how well you can maintain balance. By adopting healthier habits and committing to work-life integration, you'll not only improve your personal well-being but also find greater clarity and focus in your entrepreneurial journey.

Building Profit and Purpose Anywhere

"I always dreamed of building an international business," I often tell myself when I look back at how this journey began. For years, I carried this dream quietly, wondering if it was ever truly possible. Every time I traveled to a new country, whether it was somewhere in Asia Pacific, China, or the Middle East, I was captivated by the variety of products, the richness of culture, and the incredible opportunities for international trade. I had an unspoken love for it, but I wasn't sure how to fit it into my life.

Like many of us, I settled into what seemed like the safest and most reasonable path—a career my law degree could provide. I worked in prestigious firms, held respected positions, and followed the trajectory expected of me. And while those jobs were good jobs, they weren't really *me*. I felt a yearning for something different, something more aligned with my dreams of international business and freedom.

The pandemic changed everything. It taught me a lesson I can't forget—time is limited. Tomorrow is not promised. Suddenly, the idea of spending more years in a life that didn't resonate with who I was became intolerable. Why do we settle for less when we could pursue what truly calls to us? I realized that waiting for the perfect moment, the perfect opportunity, was just another way to avoid the discomfort of change. And I knew that if I wanted to live the life I'd dreamed of, I had to take action. Not someday. Now.

Recap of the Journey

This book has been about just that—taking action, overcoming fears, and creating a life that fits who you are. We've journeyed through strategies, rules, and insights designed to help you take control of your life and business abroad.

We started with the mindset needed for success—how to reject the expectations that others may place on you and truly understand your own needs and desires. We explored the practicalities of setting up a business, from navigating visa processes to understanding international financial systems. You've learned about building a safety net, understanding local and global funding options, and setting up a business in a way that aligns with your personal values and desired lifestyle. Each chapter has offered tools to help you break free from limitations and take a step toward living the life you've always imagined.

Pursue What Matters to You

When I moved to Dubai, I realized that a major part of living my dream meant simplifying my life. I initially envisioned an intricate corporate structure, mirroring the models of my previous employers—companies in Singapore, the U.S., and Dubai. I thought that was what success looked like. But it quickly became overwhelming—the paperwork, the compliance, the multiple tax systems. I learned that true success isn't about complexity; it's about creating a system that works for *you*. I closed down the Singapore and U.S. companies and focused on Dubai. This simplification allowed me to concentrate on what truly mattered—serving my clients, growing ByteBao, and enjoying the life I was building.

And let me be honest: pursuing my dream while raising four children has been anything but easy. There were sleepless nights, moments of exhaustion, and times when I questioned if I could keep going. But I learned to use these challenges as motivation. My children became my reason, not my excuse. I wanted them to see what it looks like to follow your dreams, even when it's hard. I wanted to show them it's possible to build a fulfilling life, no matter the obstacles. Whatever personal challenges you face, use them as fuel. Let them push you forward instead of holding you back.

I want you to know that the journey to pursuing your dreams isn't linear or without challenges. There were times I doubted myself, times I worried about whether I had made the right decisions. But through every obstacle, I learned something valuable. I learned to lean on my network, to simplify, and most importantly, to trust that I could create the life I wanted. And you are too.

Imagine Your New Life

Imagine for a moment that you've taken the leap. You're living in a new country, working on a business that excites you, and feeling a sense of freedom you've never felt before. The mornings are yours—maybe you're working from a sunny balcony overlooking the city, or perhaps you're spending time with your children before diving into your work. You've built a lifestyle that allows you to focus on what matters most to you, free from the constraints of a traditional career path.

This vision is within reach. It takes courage, yes, but more than that, it takes a commitment to your dreams and the willingness to take small steps every day toward the life you want. The lessons in this book are here to guide you—each strategy, each reflection, each story—all to show you that the life you want is possible.

Reflect on Your Own Journey

- What have you always dreamed of doing, but never pursued?

- What's holding you back from making that dream a reality?

- What's one small step you can take today that moves you closer to the life you desire?

Use these questions to reflect on your journey. There are no right or wrong answers—only what is true for you. Remember that every step, no matter how small, is progress.

Take the First Step

The most important thing you can do now is to take action. Don't wait for the perfect moment—it doesn't exist. The only moment you truly have is this one. Whether it's researching visa options, starting a savings plan for your safety net, reaching out to someone in your network, or simply writing down your vision for the future—take a step today. Each step you take brings you closer to living your dream.

I invite you to connect with me, share your journey, and be part of a community of dreamers and doers. Visit my website, join my community, and take advantage of the resources available to support you. You don't have to do this alone—together, we can turn dreams into reality.

Final Reflections

If there's one thing I want you to take away from this book, it's that the life you dream of is not only possible—it's waiting for you. My journey from law offices to international business was full of uncertainties, but every moment of doubt was worth it for the freedom and fulfillment I feel today.

Jenna, Peter, Farrah—their stories are reminders that no matter your background, your circumstances, or the voices telling you it's too risky, you can create the life you want. It may not be easy, but it will be worth it.

Time is finite. Tomorrow is never guaranteed. So why not start today? Take the risk, make the leap, and live the life that's calling to you. The world is full of opportunities—it's time to make them yours.

www.ingramcontent.com/pod-product-compliance
Lightning Source LLC
Chambersburg PA
CBHW021230130626
46554CB00004B/1416